MY GLORIOUS BOAZ

LET YOUR WIDOWS TRUST AND CONFIDE IN HIM

LIGIA BRUBAKER

WESTBOW
PRESS®
A DIVISION OF THOMAS NELSON
& ZONDERVAN

All Scripture quotations, unless otherwise indicated, are taken from the Amplified Bible, Copyright © 1954, 1958, 1962, 1964, 1965, 1987 by The Lockman Foundation. Used by permission.

Scripture quotations marked (NIV) are taken from the Holy Bible, New International Version®, NIV®. Copyright © 1973, 1978, 1984, 2011 by Biblica, Inc.™ Used by permission of Zondervan. All rights reserved worldwide. www.zondervan.com The "NIV" and "New International Version" are trademarks registered in the United States Patent and Trademark Office by Biblica, Inc.™

Scripture quotations taken from the New American Standard Bible® (NASB), Copyright © 1960, 1962, 1963, 1968, 1971, 1972, 1973, 1975, 1977, 1995 by The Lockman Foundation. Used by permission. www.Lockman.org

WestBow Press books may be ordered through booksellers or by contacting:

WestBow Press
A Division of Thomas Nelson & Zondervan
1663 Liberty Drive
Bloomington, IN 47403
www.westbowpress.com
1 (866) 928-1240

Because of the dynamic nature of the Internet, any web addresses or links contained in this book may have changed since publication and may no longer be valid. The views expressed in this work are solely those of the author and do not necessarily reflect the views of the publisher, and the publisher hereby disclaims any responsibility for them.

Any people depicted in stock imagery provided by Thinkstock are models, and such images are being used for illustrative purposes only. Certain stock imagery © Thinkstock.

ISBN: 978-1-5127-9682-7 (sc)
ISBN: 978-1-5127-9684-1 (hc)
ISBN: 978-1-5127-9683-4 (e)

Library of Congress Control Number: 2017911542

Print information available on the last page.

WestBow Press rev. date: 08/10/2017

To all those who eagerly wait for the resurrection of the saints.

CONTENTS

A NOTE

For as long as I can remember, my prayer has been that God would use me as a lighthouse. I prayed that He would use me to mark His presence and active involvement on this earth in a way that would cause others to see Him. The only problem with God is that He actually listens to our prayers; sometimes I wish He would not. But He does. And so, in order to fulfill my prayer, He brought me to the dark place of utter emptiness and nakedness, where lighthouses are needed. There is no darker place than the valley of sorrow of death. He is our Light.

My life as a teenager-orphan and as a very-young-widow contains no traces of human tenacity to handle the unpredictable. I did not do anything to deserve to be saved or led by Him. In other words, this book is not about the shared glory between God and me, a human. This book is about Jesus, the One who was able to lead me through the darkest times of my life – sometimes, in spite me fighting His inescapable grace; Jesus, the One who dear Spurgeon refers to as "our glorious Boaz".

I have no pretense of bringing into light a great intellectual discovery, or a recipe for success. I am writing out of my failure. I am writing out of my weaknesses and sufferings, which have forced me to look at the Cross.

Please don't read this book hoping to find a quick cure for the pain you are going through. I am aware this book might disappoint, but there is no pain-cure in it. What I hope you will find though, is the Person who's faithfulness and kindness shines throughout the pages of my life; it is Him, our glorious Boaz, I hope to introduce you to.

I have tried to keep the references to my personal experience in a language that portrays what God's redeeming hand looked like in my life rather than boring you with my private struggle; I am not interesting enough as a person to write a book about myself. My victory and my resurrection in Christ were not my doing, so I do not deserve any congratulations. It was all His hand at work in my life; all the glory rightfully belongs to Him. As I said in the beginning, this book is not about the shared glory between Him and me; it is all about Jesus. He, who came from above, is above all things.

I pray that you will be blessed and encouraged as you read this book. I pray that the Word of God will shine a light as strong as the one that shone in my life, in spite of my words being insufficient and unable to explain the magnitude of His grace. I pray that the wisdom of the Holy Spirit will descend on you and guide you, bringing words of encouragement and comfort in your life, bringing fruit beyond what you can imagine at this time.

Ligia

INTRODUCTION

Once death happened in the Garden of Eden, the glory we were dressed in faded and pain became impossible to avoid. *Ignoring our emotions* does not make pain go away, though it may cause us to grow cold. *Focusing on our pain* does not bring healing either. *Looking for a quick fix* to our pain, according to the ways of our instant-solution culture and struggling to liberate ourselves from pain by our own efforts is not efficient either. Trying these ways to deal with pain might harden our hearts as we miss out on a great opportunity for reconciliation between us and our glorious Boaz.

Although everyone says time heals, in my experience time *by itself* does not heal. It is what you do in the time that passes by that can bring healing or even greater pain. Time is, if you wish, merely the skin that covers a wound which may be healed or not. There are people who allow time to pass but do not deal with their pain and under the thin layer of skin there is a real wound, unhealed, full of blood and pus. Any "solution" for dealing with the pain other than bringing it all to God amounts to futile effort.

There are two reasons for writing a book like this.

The first reason is that we do not teach enough about dealing with death, and many times the process of healing that the widow(er)s in our churches go through is left in the shadow. We simply do not talk about it. Lack of information and shared experience, lack of knowledge among God's people leads to destruction, as the Bible teaches us in Hosea 4:6. No one likes to remember the pain they went through, but God's powerful hand intervening in our lives leaves a trace of blessings that needs to be shared to produce faith in others. We are a body; one body. We are knit together in love and love cares so we should care for one another. If the understanding I have received about God's hand in my life can be used by others in their walk of faith, praise God! Any work of His hand is a treasure and treasures are of no worth unless they are brought into the light and shared. If all the widow(er)s were to teach one another how to walk with Christ through pain and suffering, we would have an army of teachers that hell would be afraid of. We have in us the Holy Spirit as the greatest gift we received from the Father to help us overcome our pain, yet many of us choose to bury our pain and keep silent about it. My heart is set against keeping silent about the work Christ is able to do in a widow(er)'s life because we are not called to silence but to teach everything He has taught us!

The other reason for writing this book is that if we allow the root of the pain to be treated, not only do we experience a dimension of precious godly healing that we couldn't experience any other way, but the purpose of our existence as widows / widowers ceases to be solely reaching a certain degree of healing. Healing is a necessary first step of a long journey. If we walk the journey towards Christ instead falling on the track of a journey towards healing, healing will not become an idol or a purpose in life. The "thing" we pursue and the "thing" we are after has to be Christ, whether we are in a season of being married, widowed or single in our lives. When we cease pursuing Christ and we start chasing the healing, we stop being defined by our born-again nature and we become defined by a circumstance in our life; the Scripture calls that "idolatry".

Regardless the circumstance of our widowhood, in His unspeakable grace, God does not waste our pain. He uses the painful circumstances in our life to deal with deep fears that are only revealed when our hearts are split open. Sadly, a funeral of a close loved one can split the heart in a way that nothing else does. After healing there is a new life, a new life which might be radically different from what we thought it will be, but it is nevertheless real. We cannot allow ourselves to be trapped by circumstances and tossed around in purposeless and fruitless spirals of thoughts, because Christ did not die for us so that we would become paralyzed. His death triggered the unstoppable power of resurrection to invade the Earth and to become available for us to grab even in our widowhood. The desire of my heart is to help you look beyond the healing. There is so much to do for the Kingdom!

I am fully aware that the first section of the book might seem a bit too dry, due to the slightly theological approach. I have to admit that initially I was a bit concerned about inserting a section about God in the Old Testament right at the beginning of the book. But in my humble attempt to help you take hold of the healing that is offered by the Father and move towards the new life that follows, I will kindly ask you to take your eyes off your pain for the reading of the first few pages of this book. The detour that I believe I should take you on prior to dealing with the practical issues of bereavement in our own life might seem strange at first glance, but having buried my father at 15 and my husband at 25 and having had a few friends who had untimely deaths I have learnt that without understanding what actually happened when we broke up with God in the garden of Eden, pain is incomparably greater and complete healing is practically impossible.

The structure of the book is as follows: the first chapters of the book are linked together in a section entitled "Know the Fields You Glean In" because we will focus on the perspective God has on the current spiritual status of humanity. The concept of a "spiritual status of humanity" might seem abstract, unrelated to us and irrelevant when our heart is burning with pain in the aftermath of a funeral. But since we are part of this humanity, the definition that our culture has attributed to God greatly influences our perception of who Christ, the Father and the Spirit are, and what our God's attitude is towards human suffering. It is important to understand that death and pain were never God's intention. Also, it is important to understand that physical death is the consequence of the spiritual death we experienced and that at this point in history, it is impossible to be born without being dead spiritually – and the proof of that is the fact that we all die physically. Just as Ruth faced the challenge of taking life-changing decisions soon after her husband died, so we after the funeral of our loved one wake up in a *new reality* that challenges us to extreme. My hope is that this first section of the book will shed light on what this reality is like, both in the spiritual and natural realm.

The second section is entitled "Separate Your Harvest" because it deals with the fruit of our hearts during seasons of mourning. Our reactions to dire circumstances speak the truth about what is going on deep down in our hearts. Having the ability to hear and listen to what these reactions speak about us is more precious than gold. Separating the good fruit from the bad leads us to two key conclusions: first, it gives us an insight into the quality of our friendship with Christ; second, it provides a great distinction between what God is asking of us and what we believe we should do (influenced by the culture we live in, our own independent desires or the enemy's voice). Having been armed with this precious information about ourselves, we can then walk in freedom towards healing and far beyond healing towards helping others to heal. This section of the book also tries to provide the Scriptural resources we need to get focused (or refocused) on Christ. As Ruth chose her God in spite of her religious inheritance and her nationality, and by choosing Him she implicitly chose the fruit of her life, so we can also choose God's will for us even in the midst of our pain, by distinguishing His voice from the voice of our culture and that of our flesh.

The third section is entitled "Let The Blood That Is Water Be Water" because it refers to the social shifts which the widow(er) all too often encounters soon after the funeral. Like Ruth who experienced rejection from the one who had the right to redeem her (but by faith and obedience she was redeemed by Boaz), we have to learn to look to Christ – our glorious Boaz – as our hope for redemption and restoration. In Ruth's case restoration came from Christ through a man that He chose for her (the cultural norms of the place would have chosen someone else who was unworthy to be Ruth's partner). For us, our redemption will also come from Christ, but not necessarily by the means of what the cultural norms are – and not necessarily through a new marriage. Ruth's rock was Christ, the Glorious Boaz, not a man. Our hope for redemption is Christ, not a new wife or a new husband.

You will notice that throughout this book I emphasize a lot the responsibility we have towards God and the importance of taking decisions and not allowing ourselves to be dragged down a coil of unfinished thoughts and actions. The context in which I emphasize the need for widows(ers) to be determined is not the context of taking matters into our own hands or taking control over the parts of our lives which are not ours to control. If there is one thing we cannot do, is to save ourselves. Regardless the progress we will make as humans, we will never be able to find another way to salvation but Christ, the Lamb who was slain for us. Salvation is entirely Christ's work; we did not deserve His inexplicable grace, we did not deserve His unconditional love and we do not deserve to be called God's "fellow workers". But as "fellow workers", we actually have work to do. Our decisions actually make a difference in our fruitfulness; we can be slow at working with Him, or quick to position ourselves in the place where He may produce through us the most fruit. It depends on us how long it takes for our minds to be renewed.

Be blessed as you find your healing in the arms of the Father.

PART ONE

Know The Fields
You Glean In

CHAPTER I

OFFENDED AND AFRAID

THE CONSTANT GOD AND THE THUNDER-LIKE DEATH

In 1 Chronicles chapter 12 verse 38 to chapter 13 verse 14 we read about one of the most obscure deaths in the Bible. It is hard to understand why in a season of full joy, when the children of Israel finally behold their king who was elected and anointed by God, God kills a person during the procession of bringing the Ark of the Covenant back.

The Bible teaches us that God is good, slow to anger, loving. How does a loving God kill a human being? The God of the Bible doesn't seem to be the moody god who kills us randomly, without reason, for the enjoyment of it.

God is holy, and that is the foundation our salvation stands on. But the reverse side of the coin is that his holy and loving existence kills the sin that is spreading like a plague, be it a sin of omission or a sin of commission. In the case of Uzza, there was a clear warning that he and his blood-brothers will die if they touch the holy utensils used in the Temple. Likewise, Adam and Eve knew they would die if they ate from the tree of knowledge of good and evil.

1 Chronicles 12:38 - 1 Chronicles 13:14 (excerpts):

"All these, being men of war arrayed in battle order, came with a perfect and sincere heart to Hebron to make David king over all Israel; [...] And

they were there with David for three days, eating and drinking [...] for there was joy in Israel.

David consulted with the captains of thousands and hundreds, even with every leader.

And David said to all the assembly of Israel, [...] Let us bring again the ark of our God to us, for we did not seek it during the days of Saul.

And all the assembly agreed to do so, for the thing seemed right in the eyes of all the people. [...] And they carried the ark of God on a new cart [...] And when they came to the threshing floor of Chidon, Uzza put out his hand to steady the ark, for the oxen that were drawing the cart stumbled and were restive. And the anger of the Lord was kindled against Uzza, and He smote him because he touched the ark; and there he died before God.

*And **David was offended because the Lord had broken forth upon Uzza; [...] and David was afraid of God** that day [...] so David did not bring the ark home to the City of David [...]"*

Up to the 12th chapter of the first book of Chronicles, we read a long list of names, a brief mention of Saul's death and David's coronation followed by yet another list of names. The 13th chapter suddenly focuses on this very peculiar incident and from this chapter on something changes in the way David relates to God. Up to this point, God showed goodness and grace towards David; He rescued him many times from his enemies. But now God has an unexpected "violent" reaction. In order for David to be the king that God wants him to be, he needed to discover something new about his God, (and so did the nation of Israel): **God is constant**.

David was a very perceptive man and in his relationship with God he always shows willingness to learn and to repent quickly; he is pursuing God with an impressive persistence, being completely anchored in the God whom he dedicates his entire life to. In spite of all circumstances that he went through – being chased by Saul, sinning against others and having to deal with the consequences of others sinning against him – he did not let go of the One he loved. David is faithful in the most painful moments of his life and has a healthy fear of the Lord that represents one of the fruits of his walk with God.

However, on this particular occasion, David and the entire people act with naivety and casualness and omit the essence of what they were about to bring back among them; they were not bringing back a box, but the presence of the Holy One and according to the law, God's presence among His people always required proper preparation because in the absence of this preparation, the human sinful nature cannot stand in God's presence without being killed.

In Numbers chapter 4 v.15, 17-20, God had given specific instructions about the Tent of Meeting and the movement of the Ark of the Covenant but in spite of knowing God's laws, the men David took with him to collect the Ark drew near to it without appropriate preparation (rather than allowing the current priest - Abinadab - and his sons to bring the Ark to him, according to the law). They placed the Ark on a new cart, but God specifically forbade the Ark to be placed on a cart, old or new. It was meant to be borne upon men's shoulders - (Exodus 25:12-14; Numbers 7:9), using the poles designed for that specific purpose. In addition to this, they exposed one of the sons of Kohath to the sin of touching the most holy things.

God's motives in giving the law were not rooted in Him being picky, fussy and unwilling to dwell among His people; on the contrary, His law was given *because* He wanted to dwell among His people. He had the genuine desire to develop a relationship with them while being fully aware that they could not stand His holy presence since they were born in rebellion and sin, so He spoke out His heart; He expressed Himself. God's self-expression is what the Law is consisted of. In other words, the Law is the spoken essence of God, not a set of traps that are set by God for His people to fall into. The Israelites needed to be taught how to approach God without being consumed by His holiness, and Uzza disregarded the warnings of the Law so he died. In this sense, although Uzza's death is often used as a winning argument in debates about God's "faulty" character, this approach of understanding the text is lacking substance because it is interpreted in isolation from the rest of the Scripture. Rather, Uzza's death represents the consequence of sin coming in contact with holiness. God cannot not consume sin, just like rain cannot pour without watering the soil. (The rain cannot be accused of being mal intended towards the soil. It is a reaction: dry ground reacts to rain by getting watered; sin reacts to holiness by being consumed.)

Although they were walking with God for generations by now, the people of Israel were still, in a spiritual sense, at the beginning of their walk with Him because they were failing to see God's heart behind the Law; they were looking *at* the Law, rather than looking *in* the Law. They were not aware of the vast implications of God's holiness. But God knew who He was and He knew the effects of His perfect and holy presence among a people that were unclean and sinful. The Law existed due to God's desire to encounter His people in a way that was safe for them. That was the reason why He gave them the cleansing rituals, the rituals of preparation and all the other rituals through Moses; it was because He loved them and wanted to keep them alive as He walked with them that He gave the Law. He did this for rebuilding His relationship with them and eventually with all humanity, a relationship which was broken by humans in the Garden of Eden.

In other words, Uzza's death is neither a consequence of God being centered on Himself nor a consequence of Him being fussy about the outward appearance of fulfilling the law; it is the proof of God's unshakable drive to be with His people, love them and offer Himself to them as the Constant One, the Unfailing One, the Holy One on whom they can surely rely, since He is holy, unable to compromise.

God does not change according to circumstances, feelings or seasons. In His Kingdom, He changes the circumstances, the feelings and the seasons according to His will. He generates everything. Everything depends on Him, not vice-versa.

The constancy of God (either we are in His will or outside His will, in joy or sorrow) has dramatic implications for the creation and for our relationship with Him.

Because He is constant, all His attributes are constant, all the time. There is not one single second that He changes who He is. He is who He is! God's purity is constant because He is constant. God's will is constant because He is constant. God's love is constant because He is constant. God's heart for us is constant because He is constant. God's Word is constant because He is constant. God's promises are constant because He is constant. God's salvation is constant because He is constant. Ultimately, our relationship with Him is constant because He is constant – we are not! And grasping the revelation of God's same-ness regardless of seasons is crucial to our relationship with Him especially in this age when we try to humanize everything and we perceive Him through the murky glass of the lies the enemy has told us about Him. It becomes obvious why it was vital for the entire nation of Israel to understand once and for all that He is not shifting and that it is they who need to shift their hearts in relationship with Him. Historically speaking, under David's kingship the nation reached a period of political stability; they needed to know what – or rather, Who – they were relying on to keep the peace over the kingdom after all the turmoil they had been through. In more ways than one, their relationship reached the opportune time for God to reveal that whatever they had learned about Him and about His way of working up to this specific time in their history was not because they were special, but because He was constant. God did not protect David because David was special; David became special because God has chosen to protect him and to make him a man after God's heart. The people of Israel, they became special because the constant God had chosen them for the sake of His Name. As a nation, they flourished under His Name; they belonged to Him. That was why their enemies were God's enemies. But He warns them multiple times that His hand will be also against them if they choose to rebel against Him by following the ways of other nations. As much as it hurts Him for them, He is constant in uprooting rebellion for the love that He has for the rebellious ones. He simply loves them too much to allow them to be in rebellion, so He brings them back even if it hurts them; even if it hurts Him to do so. After all, it was the Spirit of steadfastness and immovability which generated the "I AM" name that He revealed Himself by.

If God had not been constant in keeping His side of the law in spite of all the side effects generated by it in an unclean world, the children of Israel would have learned that He sometimes does not keep His word, hence he sometimes is not "I AM". But the Kingdom of God does not rely on the economic power of a nation, on the number of warriors, on the good political counsel or on the bravery of the armies – it relies on Who God is and on Him *always* being who He is. He is the Foundation; the Son is the Cornerstone. And the Kingdom of God was to emerge from David's kingdom, as He has promised, so that the DNA of relying on God as a foundation for the kingdom was intentionally and continuously impregnated by His hand in His people throughout their history. His integrity and constancy, His unchangeable Word is what the entire promise and fulfillment of salvation stands on. It is the essence of Who He is; there is no disharmony between the way He describes Himself and Who He is, which is exactly why we can trust Him. If He had not allowed the consequences of Uzzas' sin to unfold, He would not have proved Himself to be worthy of the Israelites' trust, nor of ours indeed; if He had failed at least once in keeping His word, what guarantee would we have today that He always keeps His words and His promises to us, especially since the enemy tries to present us proofs of His lack of involvement or capacity to keep His promises?

He cannot not fulfill His side of the Law because the Law is not a set of rules that He can choose to play by or not. He is not outside the Law. The reason why we can choose to go by the Law or not is because the Law is outside of us and we are outside the Law – and part of the Holy Spirit's ministry is to write this Law on our hearts through re-birth, so the Law becomes internalized. It is not like that with God. The Law is who He is and He cannot be who He is not. He cannot choose sin because everything He does and is, is holiness, hence Law. The Law is His behavior - His lifestyle, if you wish – explained to human beings. In other words, God was not looking over Uzza's shoulder to see if he broke the Law so He could kill him. God was walking next to Uzza and Uzza's sin was consumed by God's holiness as water puts out fire.

God's presence is the antidote to sin. To eradicate a plague, all those that *choose* to bear it, against all warnings, must die. Death is always a choice, and we have all chosen to die. Not even one of us would have ever chosen God; we have all chosen death. We might think that we live outside Adam and Eve's choice, but actually, their choice to embrace death not only brought death upon themselves, but it caused the human nature to become corrupt and hopeless in finding its own way back to the Father. Human nature, outside Christ, cannot choose life any more – and the whole point of the Old Testament is to prove that to us. That is why the example of a leper colony is so relevant in the spiritual realm: we carry the disease of sin; or inner beings carry the disease of a sinful nature. God cannot abolish sin unless He kills it, for the wage of sin is death (Romans 6:23). God consumes sin by the flames of death. But in His grace, He gave His Son to die for us, in order for us to see there is another way, a way of holiness and relationship with Him. Without the cross, there is no way back to life. But if we choose life, He separates us from sin and gives us life.

Needless to say, giving up the sinful way of living is the most painful process that any human being can go through because it involves the undoing of the entire ancestral patterns of thinking we inherited, since everything we are is corrupted by sin. This is why saying that having a relationship with God is a path taken by the ones who are weak in spirit is a funny thing to say; clearly, those who say it, have never went through the pain of repentance. There is nothing more painful than being in a relationship with the God who never errs, because whenever something does not go right, you know you need to let go of your way (of thinking, being, living). Loving God is not a blissful state of mind. It is a relationship; it involves pain and willingness to change. It requires an unending humbling capacity and constant yielding to His ways. We didn't create God, God created us; hence loving God takes courage, not creativity to invent a god. We would never have imagined a pure God who changes us by confronting us with the reality of our sins. We don't even know what "purity" means unless He teaches us.

When your partner / parent / child die, you need to know Who you rely on and you need to grasp this truth with all your heart: He does not leave or change. Otherwise, none of the great promises He has for widows, orphans, foreigners or the afflicted are safe to rely on. In fact, the core of our own salvation is utter stupidity if He changes.

However, David has not had the insight into God and Law that we have now. So looking at his reaction to Uzzah's death, we notice he does not expect God to spoil the "viral party" he initiated for Him. David's intention is a noble one – to bring God back among His people, where God obviously wanted to be; and to establish God back where He wants to be. But since God does not seem to be reasonable and submit to the methods they try to implement in transporting Him, nor does He cooperate with them, David feels "offended" and "afraid" and changes his mind about having the casket of God within his city. In fact, he does not know how to handle a box full of God and he is scared that he might die as well! The king must have felt really embarrassed in front of his people.

Death triggers so many different reactions in us. We were not created for death, we were created for life. So we are puzzled by death and we surely do not know how to react to it, which is why we start asking questions about it as soon as it affects us.

Chapter 14 (verses 1-3) sheds a light on David's heart as God blesses him in spite of him being puzzled and not knowing how to interpret God's reaction from the previous chapter. The chapter starts with a great blessing:

"And Hiram king of Tyre sent messengers to David, and cedar timbers, with masons and carpenters, to build him a house. And David perceived that the Lord had established and confirmed him as king over Israel, for his kingdom was exalted highly for His people Israel's sake. And David took more wives to Jerusalem, and he became the father of more sons and daughters."

David finally gets it: what confirms him and establishes him as a king, what exalts his kingdom is the faithfulness and unchangeableness of God, the *exact same trait* that killed the one who took for granted His presence and disregarded His Law. Standing on God's faithfulness

David feels safe to expand – and another list of names follow, a list of the names of his sons and daughters. Starting with verse 10 of the same chapter, more battles follow and we see David constantly seeking God's counsel. Consequently, after going through this dramatic experience with God, in chapter 15 verses 25 and 26 we see how David's heart is changed and how aware he is of God's constancy: he makes proper preparation, he commands the Levites to follow the cleansing rituals and the transportation requirements of the Law strictly. Finally, he manages to bring up the Ark of the Covenant to Jerusalem because this time, God's presence is safe:

"So David, the elders of Israel, and the captains over thousands went to bring up the ark of the covenant of the Lord out of the house of Obed-Edom with joy. And when God helped the Levites who carried the ark of the covenant of the Lord with a safe start, they offered seven bulls and seven rams."

God did not allow the Israelites to take Him for granted in their joy because in times of need they had to be able to rely on Him and take Him seriously. And David understands that, after seeing God's hand preventing them from using their own methods in having and holding Him. God will only enter into a relationship based on purity, so He had to purify the people of Israel. For our generation, the good news is that in spite of our inability to purify ourselves, He provides us with the means of purification through the blood of His Son. We do not purify ourselves, He purifies us, but we need to be willing to be purified. We will not change Him, He changes us.

Our God is a jealous God in joy or sorrow. He is the same in joy or sorrow. He takes holiness seriously, in joy or sorrow. He confronts us with our sins because He loves us and wants us back. He is radical in His love, and unless we are willing to accept His radicalism and throw away any preconception about what we think He should do or be like, we are not in the place where we can taste the richness of His glory; He loves, He cleans, He imparts Himself. His unshakable love is not a punishment; it is the only safe ground that we can build on. We will be loved even if we hate it, because He decided to love us and there is nothing we can do about it. And if we fall out of

His will in our rebellion as far as reaching the point where His love means pain for us because we go against His hand, He will still love us until every single bondage of sin that clings to us and entangles us (Hebrews 12:1) will be eradicated from us, even if it means that pieces of our flesh fall with the bondages. He would rather have us with Him, wearing the scars of love, than away from Him wearing the scars of rebellion and wrath. It is the radicalism of who He is that makes Him our refuge, our tower and our never-failing hope. That is what makes God worthy of our trust: He did not spare anything to prove His love. Not even His Son. God's hand is not against us, He is for us. God's hand goes against sin and rebellion because sin and rebellion go against Him; rebellion is the counter-movement which goes against love, which is why there is struggle and pain in it. Love is secure and goes in a precise direction; it never fails. It is only when we join in rebellion and sin that His hand is against us. If we stay in Him, He stays in us, and His hand is for us whatever comes.

God was teaching the Israelites that He is the Rock that the Kingdom is built on. Likewise, we need a rock that we can build our lives on – we might think we are independent and need nothing to build on, but the truth is that unless we choose to build on God, we will build on something else that we see as being reliable: our relationships, our friends, our money, our social status, etc. But whether we like or not the shape of the Rock who God is, He is still the *only* rock – everything else fails. We need to learn to mold ourselves and yield our hearts to Him, because He will not change. Praise God for not changing! Praise God for not changing even if His constant character offends us or scares us as it did David. If we learn to hear His Words and apply them in our lives, His Words change us and His constancy will not offend us or scare us any longer; His unchangeable way of being will become the greatest blessing of our lives! – and especially when we go through the valley of the shadow of death, it is vital to know that He does not change! He still loves us, His Word is still true, He is still our Father, He will still keep His promises.

THE WONDERS

As a consequence of God being constant and His ways being as far from our capacity to understand as heavens from earth, we cannot have an explanation for everything that happens in our lives. The truth is, we will have questions, and sometimes, we will not have the answers. In fact, probably for the most difficult questions we have we will not find answers. Nevertheless, God does not despise our questions and He does not take away our capacity to question what happens in our lives because it is only natural to wonder why things happen in our life, as it was natural for David to react to Uzza's death.

How much time do we invest in finding an answer, though? Are we supposed to allow our minds and hearts to be consumed by questions? If we focus on finding an answer to an obsessive level instead of focusing on Jesus, we end up not only losing our partners but precious years of our life that never come back. It can easily lead to chronic depression. That is a form of abusing our capacity of understanding and it is a form of defying God. It is not sinful to ask, it is sinful to stop trusting due to the lack of answers.

If we base our acceptance of God's will and we trust in God only after we understand all His reasons, we will never trust Him. We trust Him because He does not change, not because we understand Him. His ways are always above ours. We have to learn to worship Him, not His capacity to heal or resurrect. We need to learn to trust Him *always* to take the right decisions even though His decisions might not *seem* right to us, knowing that He is *constantly* loving us.

The devil will try to use every single event of our lives to direct our focus on anything other than Jesus. We can do the greatest deeds but if Jesus is not the reason why, everything is meaningless. Every single event of our lives and every single deed that we do – eating, drinking, singing, crying, giving birth, burying, hurting, rejoicing, relocating, learning – produces fruit. If our actions are carried on as we focus our eyes on God, we will produce godly fruit. If we focus our eyes on anything else, we produce whatever we fix our eyes on: bitterness, disappointment, madness, folly or sin. The devil does not care what we look at or what we produce – as long as it is not Jesus, he will have a bountiful harvest.

Do not allow devastation to blind you. Do not allow sorrow to overcome you. Do not allow the devil to paralyze and hold you in the dry place of useless wondering. Do not fall in the trap of looking for an answer in any alternative form of spirituality or seek answers in such alternative spirituality.

Yes, we are welcome to ask God "Why?" if we want to – he is our Father, we are invited and encouraged to have conversations with Him – we are accepted by Him and wanted and expected by Him to call upon His Name. He is quick to help. He wants us – He wants us even more than we want Him! But our focus should always be on the Person that we ask the questions, not on getting the answer. There is a great difference in obsessing over getting an answer or having questions and accepting that we will never know some of the answers and moving on in trust and faith, in spite of what we do not understand. At the end of the day, if we do or do not find the answers to the *why?* questions we may have, that does not change what we need to do in our relationship with Him: accept or reject His will. He might well answer our question explicitly, but His answering is no guarantee that we will accept the answer.

God is constant even if His constancy is painful to us – but it is the rock of our salvation, the firm foundation we stand on; it is not a punishment.

FROM GENESIS TO REVELATION, A HISTORY OF PAIN

In Genesis, there are mentioned several characteristics of God that are of vital importance when the problem of pain and suffering is to be considered. It is also important to bear in mind that God is *not* limited to these attributes, but it is these aspects of His personality that are of great relevance in the particular case of pain caused by death.

The book of Genesis starts with God being the Creator. This

Creator reveals the truth about creation. Everything He created was designed in accordance with His nature. God's nature (which generates His lifestyle, His character, His actions) is holiness and perseverance in holiness. When God says His Name, He basically says that not only He possesses these characteristics of purity and holiness; He is the generator of them. Education and ethics fail and reach their end when the ones who were trained to practice them reach the point where the outcome of making "an exception to the rule" is more beneficial to them than keeping the rule. But since God is the generator of purity and He was not *taught* to be pure (so He cannot know how to or desire to adopt a different way of being), He simply cannot act on different premises than holiness and perseverance in holiness.

The aspect of purity and holiness that is often left aside is the fact that neither purity nor holiness are passive. They are not states of self-contemplation in a passive sweetness and fuzzy feelings. Purity is active; holiness is active. They grow. They expand. Where there is void, they create space by expanding, and where there is impurity, they consume it, annihilate it and terminate it. This annihilation and consumption of impurity is what the Bible calls "death". When their bodies eventually break down, humans experience the outcome in the physical realm of the death that has already happened in the spiritual realm. The physical death that we all fear and that produces pain is a symptom of the great separation between God and humans, separation that the whole of humanity is born under. We are all, without exception, infected with death.

However, we cannot blame God for this infection spreading to every single human being ever born, because God created us with free will. And we were created in this way because God loves perfectly – and a perfect love gives the object of love the option to respond to it or reject it. Neither of these reactions changes the nature, the quality nor the outpouring of love. Love is not intimidated or scared by the outcome of pouring itself out on others because in its nature, love is complete and confident. Nothing adds to it and nothing depletes it.

FREE WILL – BLESSING AND CURSE

Having been created with "free will" means three things:

1. THERE WERE OPTIONS

Free will means nothing if there are no options. So the fact that the Bible tells us that we have free will implies the fact that there are choices we may consider. The option that Adam had when he was in the Garden of Eden was to live according to God's life style and by doing this, to manage through stewardship and leadership his little kingdom (the Garden of Eden) in line with God's will. Having a forbidden tree in the middle of the garden was not God's way of playing mind-games with us – it was God's grace and infinitely pure love manifested in care for us. If He had not planted a forbidden tree, it would have meant that He would be hiding from us key features of our identity and of His.

The consequence of obeying was not only beneficial for the garden and for humanity, but it was also in harmony with the lifestyle we were created to have. As individuals, we were created to live in close relationship with God from which we absorb love that never runs out, life that never ends, joy that does not deceive and purity that knows no adulteration.

The other option was to base our pattern of thinking on something else rather than God. And Adam's choice in the Garden of Eden is what we now call "an alternative lifestyle". We have not invented the alternatives; they were always there as options – we should not have embraced them back then. Once we embraced another way of living than God's way of living, we are stuck with it. Our free will is still free. But it doesn't desire holiness at all. Basically, we are not bound by the way God created us – He created us whole and holy. We have bound ourselves and we cannot liberate ourselves. A corrupt free will is a blind free will, because it is corrupt from the inside out.

In the absence of Christ's work on the Cross and God's extended hand towards us, we cannot choose; we have no option. What the enemy stole from us was exactly the capacity to exercise free will. We have the free will, but we do not have the capacity to exercise it for choosing anything else that we have already chosen in the Garden.

2. THERE WERE CONSEQUENCES

In the Garden, when God told Adam about the forbidden tree, the idea was not to tempt people. The idea was to make the human aware that it is by choice that he is in relationship with God. The idea was to make men and women aware that they desire God, they need God and that they are connected to God in a way other beings cannot be connected to Him: by free choice. Where there is no free will and there is no mutual agreement between the two parties, the mere idea of "relationship" becomes impossible. Jesus' work is the one that broke the bondage of sin, so the Spirit could come and fill us and being filled with Him, to be able to be in a relationship with Him by choosing daily to do so. In other words, we have been positioned in a relationship with Him so we could choose to be and progress in the relationship we have with Him. What Jesus achieved through His death, burial and resurrection, was to relay the foundation of a Kingdom that should have been built through Adam. The mutual covenant between humankind and God, where both parties want to be in a covenant although both know full well that there is another option, is the key to grow more into the likeness of God.

Free will is the heart-hook by which we are connected either to God or to an idol. The problem is not that we have this heart-hook – if we did not have it, we would not be able to persist into a covenantal relationship with God. The malware is not in the way we were created, but in what we decide to do with ourselves in the Garden of Eden.

3. WE HAVE TO CHOOSE

Our separation from God was an implied consequence of the choice humans made when they deliberately decided to act according to someone else's ways rather than God's. The distance that God placed between Himself and us is not the reaction of a spoiled child or of an insecure being who throws his 'toy' away when He does not get what He wants. On the contrary, it is God's only way of protecting us from His nature which consumes sin. God casting us out of His presence was a proof of His love for us, as He later explains to the Israelites on Mount Sinai.

God did not abandon humanity after the sin committed in the Garden of Eden – although if He would have abandoned us and allowed us all to go to hell (literally), He would have been just; it was due to His outpouring of undeserved grace that He has chosen to be more than just. God's plan to bring the unclean ones back into relationship with Him was spoken even before He cast out Adam and Eve from His presence in Genesis 3:15 (text which is known as the "protoevangelium"). He never intended to withhold and isolate Himself from us (reaction which we actually deserved), but He invested Himself into making us as clean as He is so that we could stand in His presence – first by giving the Law, followed by giving the fulfillment of the Law through the only one who was worthy to fulfill it, His beloved Son.

God is the author of life. He is the source of everything that is clean and pure. He is unlimited, so no matter how much impurity His presence encounters, He cannot run out of purity because He continuously generates it. We cannot stop His nature from consuming impurity, because that is who He is – and He is constant in whom He is. That is His identity. He cannot die, He cannot stop destroying the impure, He cannot lie, He cannot pretend to be who He is not in order to accommodate our sins – and frankly, if He did, we would be left hopeless.

WHAT DO WE ACTUALLY CHOOSE BETWEEN?

In Genesis 2:16-17 and Genesis 3: 1-7, we read about the woman's temptation. She had the Word but she did not actually get hold of it; she received the information but did not embrace it with her heart.

By Jesus' death and resurrection (only by His works), this is the spiritual place where we find ourselves back to: we have the choice to embrace God's words or not to embrace them.

Knowledge has two stages. The first stage is hearing – or having encountered the information; the second stage is internalizing what was heard or in other words, getting a grip of what we have heard (assimilating). It is the action of processing the information. It is only when we internalize an idea and process it that it starts to become meaningful and to influence our behavior. The more we believe it, the more it becomes part of our screening process and it becomes a factor that influences our decisions. It gains authority in the process of taking further decisions.

The process of internalizing an idea consists of allowing that idea to take a grip in our thoughts and in our interests.

If we do not find the idea interesting we do not meditate on it, we do not analyze it, we do not let it nest in our thoughts and in our heart or still less in the core of our being. We do not go back to it. And of course, one of the greatest proofs of not internalizing God's words is the wrong quotation of them. In the Garden of Eden, there was no internalization of God's words. The proof of it is that what Eve quotes as being God's word is not what He said: God never said that the human could not touch the tree. And the interesting thing about temptation is that it follows the testing, it does not precede it; the devil does not try to tempt Eve until he discerns whether she has internalized the word of God or not. The devil does not waste his energy and his time because he is limited and he knows he has a short time to work out his plots - he tests the heart and if the heart is submitted to God (and one of the ways to submit to God is by meditating on His Word, knowing it by heart) and it resists him, he flees until he finds something else he thinks the heart might give in to; then he comes to test again. The purpose of the enemy's first question is to test if it is worth investing energy in lying. He sounds like an enquirer. By his question he insinuates that he does not know the truth, hence he asks about it. Had the woman answered quoting God's words exactly, the devil would have realized that the Word has already been processed and digested by her. It is only after Eve answers, proving she did not internalize God's Law, that the devil dares to attack the character and the intentions of God because she obviously did not get the heart of God's words. If you know someone, you cannot be lied to about their character or intentions because you know who they are. Humanity failed to know God not because He did not introduce Himself, but because they took it for granted and did not take the time to internalize the Law, which is God's spoken essence. If they had really listened to what God told them, they would have realized that they already had the notion of good and evil because God has told them: evil was to disobey. They did not really have to eat from the tree of knowledge of good and evil to know it was evil – if they had internalized the Word of God, if His Words had been grounded in their hearts, evil would have remained an experience they would not have gone through. They would have not reached a level of personal and intimate knowledge of it. Eating is a symbol of assimilation, of digesting, of gaining an intimate knowledge of something. God told them that having a personal knowledge of evil was evil in itself and would bring death. The temptation was not about the fruit, but about the eating. The devil was in the disobedience, not in a piece of fruit.

Asking why the tree of the knowledge of good and evil was in the Garden is a legitimate question.

Why did God even offer us the option to internalize evil?

And how come, if we willingly decided to go our own way that God did not simply allow us to live according to our own way, without interfering?

Where is the free will if Jesus had to die to bring us back to the initial relationship with God? And why is He sending this confusing message that we are allowed to do what we want, but we have to pay if we do not do what He wants? Is it not a constraint (or even blackmail!) always to do what He wants, regardless of our own desires?

There are two laws that form the premises of the creation of humankind. We find them in Genesis chapter 1 verse 26:

"God said, Let Us [Father, Son, and Holy Spirit] make mankind in Our image, after Our likeness, and let them have complete authority over the fish of the sea, the birds of the air, the [tame] beasts, and over all of the earth, and over everything that creeps upon the earth."

THE LAW OF IMAGE AND LIKENES and THE LAW OF STEWARDSHIP

Our world was created to reflect God's world perfectly. We were created in the image and likeness of God. God's world is a world in which evil remains external and undigested, it is not assimilated; and this is what our world was meant to reflect. Unless our world reflected God's world in all its details, we would have lost a great deal of our image and likeness with Him. Our kingdom could not have been perfect in reflecting God's Kingdom, only in the context of having evil externalized from it as a conscious act, like His.

God not only externalized sin, He externalized the one who in spite of being one of the direct recipients of His love rebelled against Him. One of the highest angels rebelled against Him and as a consequence of God's essence expelling impurity, the angel was automatically expelled. The devil's plan to keep on rebelling against God after he was expelled from God's kingdom, was to attach himself and his lifestyle to our world, contaminate it with his nature and rule over it. What he was not aware of was that the very law on which our world was initially built, the law mirroring God's world, would not change and cannot be corrupted because God is *constant*. Our world still reflects God's world: it still struggles to death (literally) to reject sin. It still struggles to externalize sin, but since it *became* sin, it fights against itself. It self-consumes, like a body that carries a virulent auto-immune disease and, in fact, that is exactly what sin is! The tension that kills this world is the *unchanging nature* of God's law of the externalization of sin and the antithetic nature of sin that operates under it.

Human beings are now made of sin (sinful nature) but still live and operate in a land that is subject to the law of sin expulsion. The objective consequences of this tension materialized in the physical world are death, illness, pain, depression, bitterness, anxieties and fears. There is no way the two opposites can work together. We are rejected by our own bodies which develop allergies to psychological traumas; we are rejected by creation itself. We are disobeyed by what was supposed to be obedient to us because we were disobedient to God. By our disobedience we cause the entire creation to be disobedient to us and struggle to keep functioning under the law of mirroring that God implemented, since the only way it could do that is by disobeying the disobedient. Sadly, this system – now dysfunctional – does not work, because there is the second law, the law of stewardship belonging to humankind. This tension is the source of illness, evil, hatred and killing, everything that eventually causes death. God's image and likeness is to externalize sin – but the very agents that were supposed to reinforce that law became corrupted. We are fallen under the curse of the same spiritual laws that were meant to protect us from death and sin. If we had kept ourselves and the entire creation under the same laws being in obedience to the *constant* God, the very same laws which now divide us from God would have brought us closer to Him, not distanced us from Him. We flipped the coin and it fell on the wrong side, but we should have never gambled in the first place.

THE KEY: EAT

The spark that triggered Eve's fall into temptation is a vital issue because if we do not understand God's words or if we only partially believe them, the areas in which we fail to internalize them become the very areas we fail to be faithful in, and we fall into disobedience due to the lack of internalization of His will in those domains. The devil has already worked that out; he knows the battlefield *very* well.

There is only one difference between the heart of Eve and the heart of Mary's (Jesus' mother). But that difference is what ultimately led to God breaking back into our world. Eve did not *really* listen to what God had to say, but Mary *constantly* kept God's words in her heart and meditated upon them (Luke 20:19, Luke 20:51).

This is why it was Mary (and not another woman) that Jesus came through, because the Word of God was grounded in her heart. She had the right attitude of heart and an obedient disposition towards God.

Do not forget that God is outside of time. For Him, Eve and Mary could have as well been two women living outside of time, without anything else than a choice: the choice is to be quick on feeding on God's Words or to be quick on feeding on someone else's word. Our souls "eat" words and produce fruit according to those words. Eve was passive when the Word of God came to her; she expected it to linger in her heart without her joining in with her own will to keep the Word in her heart. Mary *meditated* on these words, and they started taking firm root in her. She was quick to hear God and to *internalize* His words. This is how we were created to be, this is what a worshiper is – and we *all* worship the person that we allow to speak words that we keep in our hearts and allow them to grow into plants and produce fruit.

What happened in the Garden of Eden with the first Adam and the second Adam in the desert was that the devil sought to see if there was any double-mindedness. If not, the Word of God could be internalized. So in the desert, as in the Garden, Satan quoted again the Scriptures out of context, in a wrong timing, with the wrong intentions. But Jesus resisted him because He had been internalizing the Word of God since His childhood, as we read in Luke 2:40:

"And the Child grew and became strong in spirit, filled with wisdom; and the grace (favor and spiritual blessing) of God was upon Him."

Since God is the generator of life, nothing that is disconnected from Him can survive. No matter how great the personal *"life-reservoir"* of a person is or how positive s/he is; everything that is disconnected from God eventually drains away and stops living. It dies. The devil knows this; so his last chance to live was to get a grip of some other living being: the human being. As he was unable to get a grip of the authentic and genuine life of God, he reverted back to his other option:

the image and likeness of God, since God Himself is incorruptible. Without a life to be attached to, sin ceases to exist; but when it attaches to human life in the hope that it will be able to grow strong enough to surrogate God, it destroys the human that it is attached to.

When Jesus came, He said He was the Word. He completely assimilated God's Word in His human life, as He was at the same time The Word. When we have Communion and we eat from the symbolic Body of Christ, we proclaim the fact that we deliberately internalize God's Word by eating it, rather than eating from the tree of knowledge of good and evil of this world. We need to internalize God's Word intentionally. Through the death, burial and resurrection of Christ the Lord, we are brought back to "point 0" in human history, spiritually speaking. Through the work of Jesus Christ we once again have the choice to internalize God's Word. (John 6:35, John 6:48, John 6:51).

Intimate knowledge of evil was brought in the world by sinning, but as shameful as that is, it had already happened in the past; *now* our choice is what we do with that awareness that we have – and that determines if the pain that we will *surely* face brings repentance, hence love, life and acceptance or if it leads to a deeper level of bitterness and alienation, which is eternal death.

Death is the plenary manifestation of bitterness, as life is the plenary manifestation of love. In the state of depravity this Earth reached, if we remove what we wrongly believe about God and if we get an accurate image of God who is Light, we face the choice of stepping into light and feeling vulnerable and exposed, or staying in the shell of what we think of as safety, but is in fact darkness. Light reveals who we are but we simply do not like who we are, so we would rather chose to stay in darkness and hurt than come to the Light and experience a new and different kind of pain, which leads to repentance. We do not know what that new pain will bring us or produce in us, but actually that is the *good pain*, the kind that brings deliverance and reconciliation with God.

God never intended to afflict us. He never intended for us to be harmed. He never intended us to die. And the presence of pain is not the proof of God's absence; it is the proof of God's closeness. God did not conceive schemes that are designed to afflict us or our family; He did not *pass a sentence* by taking away your child's life. He designed a *perfect world* with *clear laws* and *externalized evil*. We internalized evil and the consequence of it is an overwhelming state of confusion in which only God's Son was able to restore clarity. But until the full Revelation of Jesus Christ, the entire creation is suffering. Our culture is confused, our identity is confused and the very cells of our bodies are confused - auto-immune illnesses enable us to see the obvious. We have people acting like dogs, women embracing rabbits as their children, men lusting after men, feminism, genocides, cancer, lupus. The entire world lives in a state of confusion that not only invades our minds and souls; it also invades the biological realm. And that causes suffering, pain and premature death – ultimately, spiritual death causes physical death.

The consequences of living in a sinful world are still to be experienced in their bodies, by the ones who love Him. After all, Jesus did not pray that we would be taken out of this world, but that we would have our faith kept intact in spite of the reality seen in the physical realm – then He sent us just as the Father sent Him (John 17:13-18).

It is not God who is to be blamed for cancer, rape, killing, hate, pain. It is us. That is what we created. We live in a world confused and polluted by sin. Why would we expect not to experience the consequences of our own choices and how can we blame God for our deeds?

In conclusion, the way death is defined by the Bible is God's refusal to internalize sin. Anything that is not in God, dies. God does not kill *us*, He kills the sin that we are infected with by refusing to internalize it: *He does not reject us*, hence kill us at inappropriate ages. *He rejected sin*, so we live under the law of conflict which we established on Earth between God and sin. God's will is not death. His refusal to sin brings death to anything contaminated with sin because unless attached to life, sin cannot live. God is life, but He does not allow sin to attach itself to Him, even if the support vector is a human being that cannot live unless connected to God. This is where the great conflict comes from: God loves human beings and the devil loves sin. The devil attacked humankind and contaminated them with sin because God loves humans. If God had been indifferent to us, so would the devil.

God is not mean or petty and He does not look for reasons to kill people, but God's holiness by definition consumes sin and brings it to an end – it is that end that we call "death". The light that overcomes darkness does not have an agenda of chasing darkness – the only agenda of light is to shine regardless of the consequences; and darkness simply has to flee when light comes. There is no negotiation. So it is with God's presence and sin; there's no question nor negotiation – there is a spiritual law that functions inexorably; and in His love and grace, God warns His unlearned people about the spiritual reality in which they are to operate and live, to the point of making a law out of His loving request; the entire idea of having a Tabernacle and an Ark of Covenant is the foreshadowing of the love motivated and love-generating Christ to come and dwell among us. That is how serious God is about His love for us.

We live with the false idea that God is in constant fight with the devil – and that is a very effective lie that the devil speaks into our lives. But the truth is that God has already conquered and won the fight against the rebellious angel ages ago. The fight is over; there is no question as to whether God is in control or not and there is no anxiety in the hearts of the ones who walk with Him. God is Lord and King, Ruler and Conqueror. His victory is unquestionable.

The Bible says David was *offended* by and *afraid* of God. When we pay attention to Him, He makes His love for us so obvious that even if offends or scare us, He still proves His love for us.

The tension that the children of God have to live under is that although with our spirits we already belong to God's Kingdom, we received new hearts (and we can even renew our minds!), our bodies are still in the old world and we have to deal with the consequences of living in this world that is subject to decay; we have to deal with physical death, with sickness, and with sorrow.

But, the Rock of our Salvation is the Lord who is *constant* in His love. That is why even in our darkest days and deepest pain, if we choose to run to Him, He will deliver us. The circumstances might not change around us, but the pain we endure will cause good fruit to be brought forth in our lives. By allowing Him to transform us and bearing fruit for Him, we contribute to the abolition of the old world by reinforcing the New Kingdom but at the cost of bringing ourselves as living sacrifices. That is the essence of love: laying down our own lives for others who will benefit from our pain by eating the good and godly fruit it produces, and start living by hearing our faith. That is the great reward we are called to inherit, as we put on Jesus's yoke.

The practicality of this truth is, however, excruciatingly painful. There is no point in trying to deny the fact that pain is real, that it can become intense, and that we are subject to suffering. The most heart - rending sound I ever heard is the sound of lumps of mud being dropped one by one on the wooden box in which your loved one lies. The torture of standing at the edge of the grave and listen to the echo produced in the casket is almost unbearable. The sound of burying someone is the proof of our mortality, of our powerless efforts, of our condition – ultimately, of our separation from God. And no matter how many people we bury in our lives, we will never accept that sound as being natural or as being part of our life because death is not part of life. Death should have never happened. We were not created to die. This is the reason why, even though we all are aware that death will surely come, we are still not used to it. We still do not have answers for it. We are afraid of it. And it hurts.

Comforting those who go through the painful burial of a loved one still proves difficult, although we can figure out the spiritual dimension of death and its consequences in the physical realm. No one underestimates pain and although I have had my share of funerals, I still do not know what else to do than hold the one who goes through the pain of losing the one they love. Death is supposed to be painful, but we were not created to experience it.

I am not sure what you experience with God's presence in your life was whilst going through mourning. I know what happened in my life after every funeral was complete silence. It was like God was there, but did not say anything. Seemingly, that was God's answer for me, His silence. You might experience something different, but if the only answer you get is silence, do not dismiss it. Thank God for answering because sometimes God's silence is not a punishment, it is a blessing. And sometimes God's silence is the finest tourniquet He can use on a bleeding heart.

CHAPTER II

WHY BOTHER WITH GOD
IN OUR WIDOWHOOD?

There are aspects of our lives which are subject to God's general will and aspects of our lives which are subject to God's particular will. Great pain and distress come out of not understanding which events of our life are subject to which aspect of God's will. The specific will of God is included in the general will of God. The way God revealed His general will is the Bible, and the way He reveals His specific will to us is our personal walk with Him – including prayer, prophecy, Bible study, fellowship with other Christians. God's specific will for an individual will never be outside His general will. That is the reason why we are to constantly check our personal thoughts, our ethos, our theology, the prophecies and the visions that we receive with the truth we find in the Bible. The Bible is the counter-balance for everything that we think God asks us to do and is the source of fresh encounter with the Lord.

In order to go deeper in understanding what the Bible says pain is, I invite you to think of a carousel revolving at full speed; it is designed to revolve around a secure, unchangeable axis. Each chair represents one of the luring things all human beings desire: happiness, long life, health, abundance, resources; they all revolve around the axis. This axis, unchangeable in shape, form or state of matter is God, the Creator. In His presence, all desires of the human heart are met because He is the one who generates them and He is the one who sustains them. However, when human beings chose to replace the Irreplaceable axis with one of the carousel chairs, he detached all the chains from the wheel that spins on the axis and tied them to one chained chair. Tying the hope for happiness and long life, the hope for abundance and resources to the chair called money, for instance, is insane. One chair can never support the rest of the chairs even if it is tied to the axis still less if it is completely disconnected from the carousel itself. We would never allow our children to jump on an unsafe carousel, yet we teach them to live their lives in the unsafe environment of "God does not exist" which we have created.

We were not created to function outside God's existence. We were not created to chase our own happiness. We were not created to be disconnected from Him. Whenever we decide to disconnect ourselves from Him, we actually choose to connect ourselves to something else that we think we need as a foundation for our life. "If you have money, you can do anything.", I have heard so many people say. Or, "If you have information, you can rule the world." But lights go off and carousels stop. The chains holding these chairs break. And we hurt to numbness. Idols hurt.

What I call "the place of pain" is not necessarily a funeral or an illness; death and illness and corrupt human nature are merely outcomes in the natural realm of the true "place of pain", which is a spiritual state of rebellion. It is a state in which a person focuses on self rather than God, choosing to replace God (who is the axis of the carousel) with self (which is merely a chair on the carousel). This explains why rich powerful people living in the most magnificent houses and having the most attractive partners are still in a place of pain if God is not what they pursue with all their strength, although they might never experience bereavement. God coming out of His eternity, breaking through this "place of pain" into the natural realm is what we call "Jesus". The geographical presence of a physical Person on Earth is how eternal love, originating in the spiritual realm, is translated into human language: eternal and perfect love took a body and shook the Earth. Jesus' body was – in very simplistic terms – the glove worn by Love when it broke through the barrier of matter into the physical realm. In this sense, Jesus came from a realm of eternal happiness, love, joy, harmony which all revolved around the will of the Triune God. When humankind decided that this axis (God) needed to be substituted (by self or anything else), the entire spiritual realm of love, happiness, joy, harmony became ineffective producing pain and suffering in the spirit; the outcome in the natural was death, illness, evil and loss. The way to come back from all these is not by fighting the natural symptoms or by focusing on them, but by going to the root of the issue and dealing with the real cause of the tragedy: rebellion against God.

I dare to say that God is good, and pain and suffering are a consequence of His goodness. When a child is running straight towards the fire, there is no other proof of a parent's love than to snatch, grab or even force the child to the ground if necessary, to stop the child from heading towards death. A *parent* who does not love his child enough to go against the child's will when the child's behavior is self-destructive is hardly a parent worthy of that name. Why do we expect God to facilitate our self-destructive behavior, in the name of a so-called "love"?

I praise God that He does not come to pat us on the back and comfort us as long as we choose to stay in a place of rebellion. I praise God that if we choose that revolving our lives around something or someone else than Him is still better than accepting our guilt, coming clean and choose to make our lives revolve around Him, He allows suffering and pain in our lives. I praise God that we cannot taste joy being disconnected from Him. This way, the true joy of our salvation comes not from the fact that we are loved by Him to the point of our survival, but to the point of our devotion and complete availability to serve Him. The point of God's healing is never our selfish revival and new happy life in a bubble of beatitude. That is not healing, it is mere self-indulgence.

Christians and non-Christians generally react in identical fashion in regards to the question "*How* was this possible?" when it comes to explaining someone's death, because we know that God is supposed to be good, to be merciful, to do good not evil. This kind of question arises when what we feel is not good, not merciful and it might be the greatest evil that we have faced up to that point in our lives. How come in the defining moments of our lives, everything we know *about* God simply does not seem to be working? We have a list of His attributes, and we might even feel tempted to start praying with that list before our eyes and say: "You said You are good, but You just took away the one I loved. You said You are just, but an innocent person has been killed. You said You hear, but You did not hear my prayers. You say You are a Healer, but You did not heal. How can I trust You any longer, if You lied to me?"

I cannot emphasize enough how important is to make a distinction between *a person* as opposed to *a set of traits* that person has. Healing, bringing justice, hearing, delivering, these are *actions* of God, but they are not in themselves God. God generates them and defines them, but He is not limited by them because God is a person.

When someone is sick, God's *main* purpose is *not* physical healing, it is forgiveness of sins for the ones that have not encountered Him yet or growing in holiness for those that already have a relationship with Him.

When someone is depressed, God's main purpose is not bringing happiness in that person's life, it is sanctification.

When someone is getting married, God's main purpose is not an "and they lived happily ever after" story, it is sanctification.

I know this sounds outrageous, because it means that we are not God's reason to exist – but are we God's reason for existence? The Bible does not say that – in fact, the Bible contradicts that. Because it is not us who make God do things that make us happy, it is Him who draws us near to Him in a personal and intimate relationship with Him because He is God. And trying to make God do what we want Him to do is clearly called *witchcraft* in the Bible. The groups of people who are in the greatest danger of falling into witchcraft are Christians and others that have awareness of the existence of the supernatural. The ones who have no revelation of the existence of the spiritual realm rarely fall into this trap because they simply don't believe in anything spiritual, hence they don't try to influence what they don't believe exists.

In addition to this, let me clearly state that if we expect God to act *only* as a physical doctor when someone we love is ill, we do not actually worship the God of the Bible, we worship a "spirit of healing" and not God's healing power. Segmenting God and taking only one attribute that He has and amplifying it to the point where God is that attribute *alone*, actually means we worship someone else. God is complete; He is not segmented and limited by our circumstance. The ancient Greeks believed that it is impossible for a being to be defined by so many attributes in their purest state, so they segmented God into multiple tiny gods; and they worshiped a specific attribute of God in a specific circumstance, in order to get the specific answer. If they wanted babies, they worshiped the god of fertility, in order to get a baby. But do you see where the danger is? They were the ones deciding that it is the right time for a baby, they were deciding the god that they were to ask the baby from, they were the ones who did the thinking and their gods were there to carry out their wishes. And God does not identify Himself with their gods, although He is the God that gives life and can give babies if and when He wants. He sends Paul over to tell them that He is the God that they are missing. He is the only true living God and He does have all these glorious wonderful attributes, but He does not ask us how to manifest them because our flesh never chooses sanctification, it chooses the kind of happiness we have defined with our minds. God does want us to be happy, but He wants us to experience genuine, authentic happiness. And that only flows out of having a personal relationship with Him, which is why He will use any opportunity He has to bring us into a relationship with Him, not to make us happy. And if you have ever played pool, you know exactly how this works: hit the right ball that will bounce and hit the ball you mean to get in the pocket. Unlike us, God sees the entire table. Do not try to be God's personal adviser, advocate, boss or pusher. We are none of that. We are His children. Let Him be the Father and trust Him. Trust Him as a *person*, not Him as a collection of traits. Because when you do that, you are in a relationship with Him. And that is exactly what He wants. Of course knowing His attributes makes a difference and sheds light on who He is, but He did not primarily present Himself by what He does, He did not primarily present Himself by the operational methods He applies. He presents Himself as being "**I AM WHO I AM.**" – And all these brilliant and amazing features that He manifests flow from His nature. Healing and delivering and judging and being merciful and loving us flow from the fact that He is holy, not the other way around. He is who He is, hence He hears us, He heals us and He shelters us. He is not holy because He does all these things; He does all these for us because He is holy. This is vital to understand because if we do not live according to this truth, we worship an occasionally Holy God. If God is holy and perfect only when He delivers what we decide we want Him to deliver, then when He does not "perform" he is not holy and not perfect, hence He is a sinner that sins against us. That is a dangerous heresy to fall into.

God is holy and unshakable in His holiness, which is why He does not always manifest Himself in ways we wish He did. And He does not need to ask our permission to be who He is; His existence and holiness are not dependent on us, rather it is us who depend on Him. God will not come up with excuses for being who He is, He simply exists in this state of active holiness and everything else flows from Him.

If we only believe about God that He is a physician, we will not trust Him when someone gets ill because He "fails His job description" if He does not heal that person. But if healing will not serve God's purpose for that person, He simply will not bring it forth. He will not.

He does not relate to us on our own performance level – likewise, we shouldn't love Him because He can heal, we Love Him because He is God. Healing is one of the consequences of the fact that He is God; and so is death. Death is a consequence of God being God.

WHY DOES GOD SEEM NOT TO ANSWER THE "WHY?" QUESTION?

Sometimes, God seems not to answer the *why?* question; and He seems not to answer the *why don't you answer?* question either.

Without having the pretention that the list below is exhaustive, let me suggest a few reasons why I believe He never answered neither my *why?* nor my *why He is not answering me why?* questions. Again, I am aware your experience might be different and you might know exactly why some things happen in your life, but in case you don't know, let me suggest it's okay if you don't know; you don't have to have all the answers.

1. *WE DO NOT ASK TO LEARN, WE ASK TO CREATE THE OPPORTUNITY TO TEACH HIM.*

God knows me and He knows you. He knows we are human. He blessed us with creative minds and inquisitive spirits. By nature, education, career choice or formal training humans ask questions and give answers. We are created to do so. Whatever His answers would be to our questions, if we would receive them we would have a new list of questions or solutions that He could have tried before "ruining our life forever" by taking our loved ones away at "inappropriate ages" according to our human understanding. We would, of course, have to browse through those options together. While doing that, we would keep on generating scenarios and questions – *so* many questions.

When it comes to pain, humans don't seek answers. Humans seek closure. Let me suggest that closure is not conditioned by the amount of information we have, although we tend to believe so. Closure is directly and solely conditioned of the level of trust we have in Him.

We might believe we need answers, but we actually want to know the process of thinking that God went through when He allowed our loved ones to die, so we could give Him other options and somehow twist His hand and have Him "un-do" it or at least to get Him to the point where He would have to say: "Oh, you are right. I COULD have done it that way, and that would have been better. I am sorry – will you forgive me?" – and that is wicked and wrong from any angle we look at it! We actually want to be the coordinators of our own lives and have things go the way we would like them to. It might be cute when a small girl throws herself to the ground in the middle of the store because she cannot have candy, because at her age life gravitates around candy cravings. But when we do that as Christians with God, the act loses its funny and cute side of it and the Bible calls it rebellion. When death strikes, the reason for the existence of the universe is still not changing: it is still not about US. What makes God God is not the fact that He makes our life painless. God's reason to exist is not to ease suffering; He eases suffering because He is God. God does not exist for our good; He is existence itself and our good comes from His existence, as we reflect His existence. Our suffering ceases as a consequence of our proximity to Him and trust in Him, regardless of our emotions or level of understanding.

2. WE DO NOT SIMPLY WANT TO KNOW WHY. WE WANT TO NEGOTIATE.

The Bible repeatedly proves that we have an amazing ability to negotiate. I believe the most eloquent example is to be found in Genesis 18:17-33, where Abraham pleads for the sinful cities to be forgiven and the Lord to change His mind about destroying them:

<< *Then the Lord said, "Shall I hide from Abraham what I am about to do? Abraham will surely become a great and powerful nation, and all nations on earth will be blessed through him. For I have chosen him, so that he will direct his children and his household after him to keep the way of the Lord by doing what is right and just, so that the Lord will bring about for Abraham what he has promised him."*

Then the Lord said, "The outcry against Sodom and Gomorrah is so great and their sin so grievous that I will go down and see if what they have done is as bad as the outcry that has reached me. If not, I will know."

34

The men turned away and went toward Sodom, but Abraham remained standing before the Lord. Then Abraham approached him and said: "Will you sweep away the righteous with the wicked? What if there are fifty righteous people in the city? Will you really sweep it away and not spare the place for the sake of the fifty righteous people in it? Far be it from you to do such a thing—to kill the righteous with the wicked, treating the righteous and the wicked alike. Far be it from you! Will not the Judge of all the earth do right?"

The Lord said, "If I find fifty righteous people in the city of Sodom, I will spare the whole place for their sake."

Then Abraham spoke up again: "Now that I have been so bold as to speak to the Lord, though I am nothing but dust and ashes, what if the number of the righteous is five less than fifty? Will you destroy the whole city for lack of five people?"

"If I find forty-five there," he said, "I will not destroy it."

Once again he spoke to him, "What if only forty are found there?"

He said, "For the sake of forty, I will not do it."

Then he said, "May the Lord not be angry, but let me speak. What if only thirty can be found there?"

He answered, "I will not do it if I find thirty there."

Abraham said, "Now that I have been so bold as to speak to the Lord, what if only twenty can be found there?"

He said, "For the sake of twenty, I will not destroy it."

Then he said, "May the Lord not be angry, but let me speak just once more. What if only ten can be found there?"

He answered, "For the sake of ten, I will not destroy it." When the Lord had finished speaking with Abraham, he left, and Abraham returned home. >>

Christians have the biblical responsibility to use all the ability they possess "in the right way". "The right way" does not mean "the way that brings them comfort" or "helps them accomplish their goals". "The right way" means "in a way that is pleasing to the Lord" or "according to God's will" or "as God decided", and the ultimate purpose for all is for the Kingdom to come.

God created us with the ability to negotiate. He loves us. It is not a sin to negotiate and it is not a sin to ask God how we can use the ability to negotiate in a way that would be useful for our families that we need to provide for in godly ways. But when we use the abilities we have to seek primarily our own interests and we exclude God's interests, He is not impressed. That is what those that do not know or love Him do, and it is called idolatry.

How do we differentiate good negotiation from bad negotiation? When we have nothing to give – literally nothing, because we do not even own ourselves – and we cannot quantify the results of either getting or not getting what we desire and we do not really know what God's further plan is, it might become odd to negotiate with God, in the sense of "trading" with God.

Other than not trying to get something that is displeasing to God (which would make as much sense as praying for the circumstances in which you could commit a sin to come together and enable you to do so) the other criteria that applies is: are we humble enough to know and accept that He is still God and Lord if we do not get what we want? Or do we want that specific thing that we pray for more than we want to be in His will?

Do we really mean it when we say in our prayers that we completely submit to His will and abandon our desires and personal interests in order to follow His interests and desires? Do we really want Him?

Negotiation is not manipulation, blackmail or threat and reproach. We need to learn to differentiate the fruit of our pain.

If you ever find yourself sitting on a chair in the hospital waiting room, do not try to force God into acting according to your will by offering yourself instead of the loved one who is on his death bed. Do not try to manipulate God. Any attempt to manipulate God by using any kind of natural or supernatural act – including prayer! – is witchcraft. Trying to manipulate God, at its core, is witchcraft - which is a sin of commission; and it should be taken in all earnest! Do not attempt to manipulate God.

The concept of blackmailing God is hilarious for several reasons. First, He knows our thoughts so He knows when we are trying to blackmail Him. Second, we have nothing that He *needs*. The concept that stands at the base of blackmailing is that the one being blackmailed is in vital need of something that the offender has. This does not apply to humanity in relation to God. Third, if He wants something that is in our usage, He can take it. Merely the fact that we are at the burial of someone that we love so much that we are ready to blackmail God to get that person back, is the proof of the ineffectiveness of attempting to blackmail Him. Fourth, everything that exists belongs to Him. Do not say a prayer like: "God, if You do this one thing for me, I'll do this other thing for you."

People who attempt to blackmail God have a wrong interpretation of His Word, like all major heretical religious movements. We cannot quote the Bible out of context or without understanding who God (the author of the Bible) is and what He specifically says at a certain moment, and pray the "self-righteous", "holier than thou" prayer: "But God, you said that Your yoke is easy – and burying my husband is not easy. You said it, so undo his death, please!". Trying to blackmail God, at its core, is ignorance - which is a sin of omission.

Do not threaten God. Do not give Him ultimatums. Do not command Him. Do not twist His hands promising you will never attempt to fulfill His desires if He does not fulfill yours, because if that is what your prayer sounds like you most certainly have not fulfilled His desires anyway up to that point. Do not reproach God making up a list with all the things (you think) you have done for Him. Our God is not a God that counts and balances good deeds versus bad deeds – mainly because He can find fault even in angels. (In fact, it is a blessing He does not look for our faults!) God is not impressed with our curriculum vitae. Neither is He impressed with our good deeds to a point where they would stand as witnesses against Him in some imaginary trial that we might get Him involved in.

Having an attitude towards God and using a tone with Him, being furious at Him, is idolatry: the one that does it believes he is above God and God is there to meet his needs; and unless He meets his needs, He is a bad God that does not deserve the attention or praise of the lesser human-god that prays the prayer. Trying to submit God to us is wrong adoration, it is idolatry – which is a sin of commission.

The core of good and holy negotiation is not about getting something that we really want from God, but about getting to know more about His character and love Him more for who He is not for what He does for us. The negotiation process in itself is a very enlightening process because it commits both parties to listen and hear each other and care about the other's needs, wants and desires. We are blessed to have a God that hears and listens to our prayers. But we are cursed if we mistake His availability to listen with some sort of weakness that we might exploit.

3. "KNOWING" IS NOT SYNONYMOUS TO "ACCEPTING"

When death occurs, the greatest issue that a human heart deals with in relation to God is acceptance. Accepting God's will cannot be conditioned by our understanding of Him. Understanding God's ways requires grace and it fills us with peace. On the other hand, not understanding God, although it is not uncommon or sinful to bring a sense of urgency, it becomes sinful if it brings refusal to accept His will. We can never and will never completely understand God. And even if we were to agree with the reasons He had to take away our loved ones that would not bring acceptance by default; we would still be devastated and we would still have to fight to accept His will. If you take a quick look at the book of Job, you realize that he does not get an answer for his pain, other than God revealing Himself and Job developing the right attitude towards God: trust. He understands the source of his suffering was him trying too hard to understand God because understanding operates from our mere human capacities but trust operates from our relationship with God.

Knowing why someone died does not make it any easier to accept it, although it may always seem to. Our rest is in who Jesus is, not in having our emotional needs completely met. But the paradox is that when we rest in Him, our emotional needs are completely met and satisfied, although we were focusing on who He is not on getting a resolution for our emotions. Jesus had the entire world at His feet, yet He bled in prayer, preparing for an emotionally depleting and physically excruciating death; a death He did not *have* to die but He has *chosen* to. His emotional needs were not met – no one looked at Him to tell Him that He is understood or appreciated for what He did; they all cursed Him, spat on Him and wanted Him dead. The Son of God died on a miserable cross the death of the most heinous criminal and there were no arms to hold Him. There was no consolation that the abandoned Son of God had other than the trust He had in the Father's character. There is no greater example of abandonment in human history than the death of Jesus. Yet, He was named "The Beloved Son of God". His emotional needs not having been met were not a proof of God's indifference; it was a price He chose to pay to accept and fulfill God's plan.

Not having found an answer to the question of why we have buried our loved ones, even though it appears to be vital, in fact it is not. On the other hand, accepting God's will in our lives is vital and not doing so causes spiritual death. Having information does not necessarily mean responding to it (as God would have us do). The Scripture says in James 2:19b that even the demons believe that — and shudder. The demons have this information, but they do not act on it in faith; they do not accept the fruits that it should produce in their lives. They, unlike humans, have the answer to the "Is there a God?" question that has always been culturally fashionable to debate. But they are the proof that having information does not help unless that information is accepted and internalized.

We are not allowed to devote our lives or to tie our happiness to the existence of a person – yet we do it and if that person dies, we not only become sad, we may easily become obsessed with the wrong issue: knowing why. If we cast our anchor into shifting sand, there's no wonder if tides take us away into the open sea.

It might sound radical, insensitive and unfair to tell someone that has just buried their partner not to obsess over the question why – but would it be more sensitive to allow that person to sink into endless hours of fruitless questioning?

I have met a woman that used to visit her husband's grave three times a day in the hope that one day when she is there her husband will be resurrected not as a consequence of Jesus's return but as a result of her prayers. The grief in her children's eyes can hardly be expressed in words, but they, being too young to protest, had to accompany her on her visits to the grave. Those children had not only buried their father, they were burying every day, three times per day, bits of their mother and bits of themselves. That was not a proof of faith coming from their mother – it was a devastating proof of obsession using "faith" as a selfish maneuver to get what she wanted.

When Claudiu, my husband, died, too many people have asked me if I asked myself why God chose to take him. My answer was always the same: "I thought about wondering why, but I realized that knowing why would not actually help me in any way overcome the reality of his death, and I decided not to waste my time wondering why but rather focusing on what's important." I am positive that an overwhelming percentage of the people who heard this answer did not believe me. But in fact, it is true. I thought about asking God why, but I did not. It would not have helped. What I did ask Him repeatedly was if He saw what happened. I asked Him if His eyes were looking over me when I was wounded. I asked Him if He would heal me. I asked Him if He cared. I asked all those questions. And the reason why that was how my prayers sounded was that I knew the story of the woman that used to go three times per day, every day, to her husband's grave since I was a child. Everyone living in the neighborhood knew her because she bragged about it. My fear of going down the same road as that woman went was stronger than my desire to chase something that I had no means of retrieving. My stubbornness not to fall into the temptation of excavating the past was a gift that I received from the Holy Spirit which enabled me to move forward.

I later realized that, in fact, when Jesus died to stop the power of sin, He answered all my questions because by His death, He brought death to the decision we took to dedicate our world to injustice. He is not the problem, He is the solution, even if He doesn't give us answers.

WHAT WILL HAPPEN TO ME IF I ACCEPT ALL THIS AS BEING TRUE?

If you really allow God to heal you, prepare to have your eyes opened to see what healing really is. When He deals with your emotions, He deals with them completely. He just needs to receive your permission to restore your being. And someone's death is the kind of experience that is strong enough to make a crack in your walls for you to open up to Him. This is what "allow your pain to be purposeful" means. You need to understand that God just giving you tender emotions reduces God to a kid of puppy you get as a Christmas gift. Fuzzy emotions will come and follow, but they are not the reason why God exists, so they will not be the reason why God acts. God's actions are always in accordance with His nature and with who He is because there is no fragmentation in Him.

I am not saying that we should desire to feel pain nor that we should not desire to be healed; pain is real and it does hurt. Of course we want to protect ourselves from it! That is why pain is such a strong tool in God's hand that He can use for our good. But if your pain is throwing you into a spiral of despair, if your faith is shaken and if it turns your heart in bitterness or hostility towards God, there is something wrong with your pain on a spiritual level. It is an abnormal manifestation of it. The fruit should not be bitterness, depression, anxiety; it should be yielding to God in spite of your emotions. Crying is okay, if you direct it towards God, but if you turn crying into paralyzing self-pity, you have to open your eyes and understand that there was something in you that was misplaced which has been brought to light by this tremendous pain. In other words, neither extreme pain nor extreme joys are accepted as an excuse to separate us from God. And the Bible tells us that they cannot separate us from God, so if we discover that something separates us from Him, we need to be brutally honest with ourselves and bring it out in the open in prayer, if we truly desire the healing that God offers.

For every request that we bring to God we need to be prepared for Him to respond in an unpredictable way. We are not always aware of the root of the issue that causes pain or unhappiness or illness in our life - nor joy and happiness. The price we pay for anything He does or gives to us, is nothing less or more than our self-life. Our minds do not understand what He is doing, our emotions cannot contain Him. He is outside of us, He is independent, and He acts on our words of repentance and provides - *always* provides! - what we need; that is what makes Him holy and wise; He deals with the root of the issue, not the fruit of it. We need to be willing to pay that price, or our engagement with Him will be a continuous source of frustration and pain. God does not compromise His actions - neither their wholeness nor their purpose - because there is no sin or error in Him. He does not waste anything that belongs to Him or His people; He does not waste Himself. This is why we need to be prepared for Him to work deep in us, and not just superficially. The life that He brings forth is not a man-made work so when we pray for healing He does not give us instruction on how to avoid pain, He does not focus on the pain or teach us how to feng-shui our apartment but He steps right into the middle of the mess and acts on the root of the issue. He does not know how to work otherwise. Everything He does, He does thoroughly. Otherwise, what point is there in a partial fix that will not last and will need healing again when it comes out of our hearts in the shape of another fruit that is equally negative?

No one wants to face the storm, but we have already chosen to go through storms when we rebelled. Storms are just the natural consequence of our rebellion. If we know we are in the place where storms happen, there is basically only one decision we can take: face the storms going back towards our God (which is what repentance really is!) or face the storms going the same direction that got us into trouble in the first place. We will encounter storms. Do not try to live in an imaginary world without afflictions, because Earth is a battleground. Houses, bank accounts, families – these do not constitute spiritual safety, and we are spiritual beings primarily. The only healthy choice that remains is for us to live in this unsafe place *with a purpose*! We cannot break out of this place which is contaminated with death, but we can live purposeful in it. We are not called out of this world, but to walk in it holding on not to the illusion of never facing pain, but holding on to a God who actually gives purpose and makes sense out of all the mess and confusion that we have got ourselves into. He has a plan: bringing down the Kingdom!

Ideally, when the storm hit us, our relationships with God should already be established. (We definitely need to learn what means to *pray in season and out of season*.) But if there is no established relationship between us and Him yet, it is high time that we started grasping the reality of who He is and begin to walk with Him in perfect harmony, yielding every thought and intention towards fulfilling His plan.

Learn to get your joy from your relationship with Christ, if you have not learned to do so in times of peace. Times of peace are allowed in our life to enable us to focus on Him, and so are troubled times. There is no season in which we are allowed to become less intentional in our relationship with Him (2 Peter 1). When we stop going forward, we do not stay in the place we were last time - we fall back!

PART TWO

Separate Your Harvest

CHAPTER III

THE HEALING

Healing does not come by itself and it does not have a recipe. They say "Time heals any wound." but after my father died I discovered that the passage of time does not automatically bring healing. It is what we do with ourselves in that time that can bring healing or create even more damage in the long run. The passing of time is similar to a thick layer of dust laid on a piece of shiny furniture – wipe it off and the furniture will shine again. The passage of time can also be compared to a scar tissue grown on a foreign body which has not been removed from the wound. There will be puss and bleeding whenever a little bit of pressure is applied on the infected area. Unless you decide to deal with the source of pain – however scary it sounds, the cause of pain will be buried but not resolved. I want to encourage you by telling you that honestly dealing with the source of pain is even scarier that you can perceive when you decide to do so but it is, nevertheless, the only way to true healing.

Our emotions are real, our fears are real, our anxieties and hurts are real and unless we are willing to go as far as necessary to sort them out in our hearts, they will show up in the least expected ways at the least desired moments. The consequences of not dealing with pain are definitely even more devastating than dealing with it. Ignoring a broken leg does not mean that the break is undone, it just means that a serious trauma is ignored and when (not "if"!) the leg will be needed to walk on, it will hurt even more than when the break occurred.

Pain is not related to something material but it is related to the spiritual realm. The spiritual realm functions by different mechanics than the physical realm. In the physical realm, if something is broken there is a way to fix it. If a glass vase is broken, the glass can be recycled and you can get a new vase identical to the first one, if you wish. In the spiritual realm, things can never be undone by reversing what happened. You cannot fix your heart by pretending you were not married and you cannot undo death.

The depression and anxiety we might feel after burying the loved one is never caused by what is happening outside us, although it might be triggered by something exterior like bereavement or funerals. In reality, pain originates in the human spirit and it is a symptom of our separation from God. You might find yourself causing even more damage if rather than dealing with your inner pain you start dealing with the people who sinned against you, looking for justice. Yes, we might have to pursue justice and we might need to move house to enable ourselves to focus on the inner pain without being distracted by unwanted memories as a first step, but healing is a journey. Do not think that if you could find justice and see the one who killed your child imprisoned, you will be healed; you will be vindicated, but you will not be healed. Vindication does not mean healing. Justice needs to be done, without question, but your heart needs to heal independently of any of the exterior circumstances because sadly, sometimes justice is not done; if your healing is wrongly based on a vindication that never comes or any other circumstantial factor, you do not have the wherewithal to build your life from that point on. If you base your healing on having the best looking gravestone with the most flowers or the most serene funeral for your partner, what do you do if some drunk driver crashes into the gravestone and smashes it? Your heart is more valuable that the appearance of a grave, a house, a circumstance or an imperfect justice system. There is a right way to honor the memory of the lost one, of course, but your healing does not originate in the degree to which the memory of the loved one is honored; your healing originates at the Cross. Taking this step a bit further, let me suggest that it is only from a place of healing that you can reach out and improve the justice system. Without any doubt, it is only when you are healed that you can change the circumstances around you in an impartial way because it is only then that you are no longer blinded by pain or driven by the wrong motives that you can take impartial decisions. And you do need clarity of mind when you take important decisions; the risk of taking life-changing decisions in moments of panic is too great. Heal – heal truly! – and then decide what steps you need to take.

What liberates people from alcohol abuse through AA programs is the decision to go to any lengths for victory over alcohol, combined with the willingness to act on that decision. Out of that decision, people find the strength to find the right program that helps them. These are the people who honestly decide to go with the program and deal with the root of the issue. The reason why some weight loss programs are successful in some cases and are not in other cases is, again, not the diet exclusively, but the decision of the person to lose weight and the right diet for their body type. Likewise healing, surviving in dire circumstances, forgiveness and happiness; these are decisions, not states of existence determined by context. Unless you take the conscious decision to do whatever it takes (however painful!) to get healed, you will never find healing. No one can decide this for you and no one can ignite in your heart the desire to make this decision other than you.

HEALING IS ONLY TO BE FOUND AT JESUS

When God acts, He does not make us the center of attention. When He speaks and directs us, we are not the purpose of His existence. When He heals us, He heals us for a purpose other than the healing itself. God loves us with an unquenchable love, but He will never ever speak to us in a way that will make us feel that His activity gravitates around us or that we are His focal point. The center of attention is always, without any single exception, His plan. Though that might be offensive and unpopular in a self-centered post-modern culture, if He were to make any of us the center of attention, we would be crushed under a burden we would not be able to carry, which is the burden of actually becoming God.

What the Bible teaches about healing is that the only way to be truly healed is to stop focusing on anything else (be it healing in itself, pain, justice, change) and start focusing on Jesus. When we do that, we lift our eyes from the issue and we look at the solution. The Old Testament contains many foreshadowing of the work of Jesus on the cross. A relevant example is mentioned in Numbers chapter 21, when the people of Israel grew impatient with the long journey and God sent poisonous snakes against them. In verses 8-9 we read:

"The Lord said to Moses, "Make a snake and put it up on a pole; anyone who is bitten can look at it and live." So Moses made a bronze snake and put it up on a pole. Then when anyone was bitten by a snake and looked at the bronze snake, they lived.".

Lesson after lesson, God tries to teach His people not to look at the circumstance. They look at the inhabitants of the promise land and doubt God, so God sends them on a long journey to teach them in isolation what looking at Him means. But even at this stage, whilst being in complete isolation in the desert, the people look at something else rather than God: they focus on the isolation itself (the length of the journey, the food they eat, etc.); and again the people speak against God. So God has to probe deeper into their hearts because the roots of their lack of trust in Him are so deep in the soil of their hearts that even when they are walking step by step with God they focus on the steps not on God. Thus to conquer the giants in Canaan they have to learn to eliminate any distractions and focus on Him. Eventually, God sends snakes to kill them to force them to look at Him. This new lesson is exactly the same lesson as the previous one – "Focus on Me, not on your circumstance!". The only difference is that this lesson has immediate implications: whoever does not look at the snake on the pole raised by Moses dies.

When Jesus died He offered the solution to death. He was lifted on a pole and we have to learn to look at Him and we have to learn to live in the goodness of the eternal life He has already won for us on the cross. True healing comes when the pain caused by death is made subservient to the goodness of God. Only when His goodness and love for us carries more weight than any circumstance and we can anchor our emotions and our stability in His death (which is followed by resurrection), the healing process can start.

The solution for death that Jesus provided is not only a promise of eternal life for those who die in Him - as important as that is! – because we all have loved ones who live outside His promises and we cannot force them into heaven. Jesus' victory on the cross is not only a solution for tomorrow for those who died in Him, it is a solution for those who are living on earth and are mourning. It is His precious presence by our side when we go through the valley of the shadow of death. The Son of God is present and eager to hold you as you walk through the shadow land. But you need to accept this Truth with your mind and let it sink deep into your heart. It is up to you to choose the method you want to use – but it has to involve exposing your heart to Scripture and prayer. It has to involve communication between you and the Son of man. Otherwise, the bitter history of Lot's wife is likely to be repeated in your life. I think it is the most immediate example of a person being saved and not living in the fullness of salvation. It made no difference that she was outside of the area where death had power; she gave power to death over her as she leaned in her heart towards it. Healing is not a surface process, it is not about changing a house or a car, it is the inclination of our hearts. You can change your house, your wardrobe, your friends, and your job: it is not a proof of healing.

Why not make the most of being a Christian? Being a Christian is not a hobby or a social skill; it is an abundance of death-conquering, victorious life because of the death of Jesus and His cross around which your life revolves. God's presence in your life brings healing automatically. This does not mean that He wastes Himself – it is one of the most subtle but nevertheless important principles in the Bible that our spiritual gifts are to be stewarded, not wasted because our God does not waste Himself but He wisely imparts Himself. At the same time, God is not stingy or parsimonious. He invites us to come to Him and in fact, He sent His only Son to show us the way to Him. However, our hearts need to be positioned in the place where they can receive His healing. Like the woman in the crowd who touched Jesus' garment, if someone genuinely looks for healing *from Him*, healing does come by merely touching His clothes. A heart that is willing to accept that healing and starts with genuine repentance will savor the honey-like taste of restoration of the entire being.

The battleground is in your mind, in accepting that death is conquered and you are healed in that victory even before you were hurt. It is frighteningly easy to talk yourself out of God's will and out of His plan for you by choosing to see yourself as incapable of being healed, as forgotten or unimportant. You have the potential to be either your own greatest enemy or your own greatest friend.

Our new life starts with repentance. Our healing also starts with repentance.

HEALING IS NOT BETREYAL; REFUSING THE HEALING, IS

If you look at the one who passed away you will feel that any step you take towards your healing is betrayal because the last common experience you have with them is death, hence suffering. Yet your undivided devotion is not towards any other human being but to Jesus as the man and the God who saved you. You are not beholden to anyone else. You do not belong to anyone else. No other being has ever had ownership over you. No other being has any power over you. And you are the one who decided this when you decided to become a Christian. When you decided that you wanted to belong to God and you were born again, you decided that any other relationship is subservient to your relationship with Him, hence the first Person you betray or not is Christ. Even when we sin towards other people, the Person we sin against in the first place is Christ.

Of course we end up disappointed with life, but becoming a Christian does not mean that we will be spared disappointment or pain. It means that whenever we are disappointed or hurt, we will make the conscious decision not to throw God out of our lives, even if we could to re-write the story of our lives from scratch. He is the only one who can heal; if we throw Him out, we throw out our own healing.

On the other hand, refusing to heal by deciding to stay in that state of continuous mourning means that you reject God's love for you – and how else would you feel than unloved if you do not allow Him to love you? The love that you lack might be projected onto the person who died, but actually the love that is redemptive and strong is not a human love but God's love manifested to you either through another human being or directly through the power of the Holy Spirit. He is allowed to choose to love you through your partner or your child, and He is allowed to choose another method of showing His love towards you if your child or your loved one is no longer there. To begin with, if the love that reached out to you through that someone was indeed love, was not generated by that person's initiative but by God through that person. Do you trust God enough to believe that if the person who He loved you through is no longer near, He will find another way to love you, or will you reject God's love merely because His new way of manifesting His love towards you does not fit your idea of how you think you should be loved?

Refusing to walk in God's answer to human pain is nothing less than refusing to walk in God's answer for you. No one can limit the healing effects of the Cross on your pain but yourself; you alone can willingly separate yourself from the Body of Christ. Refusing to look at Christ is not devotion to the one who died; it is actually betraying the Son of God. In a shipwreck refusing to float means choosing to sink.

Betrayal and devotion cannot be manifested towards the deceased chiefly because the living and the dead no longer belong to one another. If a husband dies, his wife cannot commit adultery against him any longer because they do not belong to each other anymore. The dead are not affected on a relationship basis by the choices of the living, as the living are not affected in a relationship sense by the ones who have passed away. There are circumstances in which the living may find out details of the lives of those who have passed away but that still does not bring any tension in the relationship between the two – although it may alter the memory of the dead – because there is no relationship anymore. You cannot betray someone who does not exist anymore, even if they did exist at a particular time, they were real and they were important to you. But Jesus is alive and He did die for you and you can betray Him because you can have a relationship with Him which you can turn away from. This is why the resurrection of Jesus makes such a difference in our lives, because without His resurrection we would still not be able to be held accountable for our choice to reject or accept Him. Likewise, His resurrection is crucial when it comes to our experiencing the pain caused by a loved one's death because if our emotions and our decisions are anchored in a death which does not contain in itself the miracle of resurrection, we lose all hope for life and effectively, we anchor our life in death thereby denying the effects of the Cross over it. But if our emotions and our decisions are anchored in an unfair death which was followed by an unstoppable resurrection, we are resurrected from our pain since Jesus has been raised from the dead (chronologically, even before we were hurt).

Whenever Jesus performs a miracle of healing in the Scriptures, "Be healed!" is not a polite suggestion, a sympathetic invitation or a polite offer that He makes. God does not give us the option to choose if we want to be healed or if we think we can manage with our pain, to let it sink into our hearts. God is determined to heal. We are more than invited to be healed, we are touched by God and commanded: "Be healed!". We are more than honored to have the source of Life at hand to make the most of it and be healed. We are commanded to accept healing and to walk in the good of it – and although my position might be seen as being radical, I believe that deciding not to heal is rebellion. The reason why God commands us to choose healing is because God does not heal us merely for the sake of healing. Yes, He wants to heal us, but healing comes as a consequence of us giving up the state of rebellion we were born in. This is why our physical healing is the last type of healing we experience – He first liberates us from our inherited sinful nature (by birthing us through the Spirit), He liberates us from our own sins, He fills us with the Holy Spirit and He gives us a new direction in life (the direction of His plan). At this point, after the work of the Holy Spirit is well established in our hearts, we understand that death is still hovering on the surface of the earth because we are not alone with God. We live in a world permeated by sin and the consequences of a sinful and rebellious life on earth are still felt by those who have chosen a different path. It is only from a healed heart that we can understand the painful consequences of un-healing.

Paul reminds the Galatians that choosing freedom is not merely one option among many; it is the only option that we have other than death and by not choosing life we are still making a choice – we choose death: "It is for freedom that He has set us free" (Galatians chapter 5 verse 1). In other words, we were made free not so that we may choose captivity – we were made free so we could walk in the freedom that we have received; this freedom was not cheap! It cost God everything He had! Our freedom meant His enslavement. But for some reason, humans do choose to pay the price for their healing by choosing endless pain instead of choosing to walk in the healing that has already been provided for them on the cross. It is because of our stiff necks and proud hearts that God not only sets us free but commands us to walk in that freedom.

Unlike us, God knows that anything we nurture in our hearts grows (He is the one who created our hearts!). Any resentment, any pain, any thought that we have and hold in our hearts will increase. Our thoughts are not like phrases written on pieces of paper and filed away in our hearts our hearts. Our hearts are like an oven in which we place dough. Every thought, every secret, every pain grows, expands, bakes. It develops. God's words in us are active and produce life in us. The thoughts that we produce – the bitter, self-pitying words we speak to ourselves – not only are painful in themselves, but they multiply and produce even more words of condemnation, depression, sadness, anger and pain. In verse 47 chapter 32 of Deuteronomy,

Moses warns the people of Israel shortly before his death that God's words are not idle words but that they are life.

HOW TO LOOK FOR HEALING?

After Claudiu died, I spent some days – maybe a couple of months – looking for answers from people. Because I am a thoroughgoing introvert I did not reach out to connections. I reached out on Christian forums for widows. I had just turned 25 when Claudiu died. Everyone else on these forums was over 40. They were at different stages in life and in different places in their walks with God. I did not write anything, I just browsed and read theories about pain, death, lamentations on forums, and (sometimes really bad) advice. So one day I just stopped, thinking to myself: "This is crazy. This will not work. If I want God, I need to go to God."

So my first practical step towards healing was looking for Jesus. I did not know what to do or what to read; I just went to the Scriptures. I allowed the Holy Spirit to guide my reading, to guide me back to the Scriptures that were spoken over my life so many years before.

Looking for healing is nothing other than looking for Jesus. Healing comes as a consequence of our encounter with Him. In my journey, healing meant that I spent countless hours in prayer and countless hours reading the Scripture. But my starting point was not a ritualistic prayer time or a decision to read a number of chapters from the Scripture each day. There was nothing forced in my walk towards Jesus. There was only grace from Him and willingness from me.

I started exposing my heart to the Scriptures and I started listening to sermons from sources I knew were godly; not all so-called information out there is reliable. In my search for "spiritual food" in sermons, I had to start looking in the Scriptures even deeper to check if what those people were preaching was in accordance with the Scriptures. My prayers were very simple, extremely child-like. I connected to Him. I started pursuing Him and I started looking for a relationship with Him. I started talking to Him because He was the only one who did not abandon me. I know that my friends did not want to abandon me and there is no condemnation for what they did; they got scared of the storm to the point of running and they ran. I would have run as well if I could have – but I could not. This was *my* life; it was happening *to me*; it was happening *in me*; I was breathing it and seeing it and hearing it. I had to fight the fight even if I would have traded anything to be given the choice to chicken out. But I was not given any opportunity to be a coward. Courage was not an option that I took; it was the only option open to me. By pressing through and breaking beyond the circumstance, I was able to find the strength that He gives. When our strength is enough, we do not see miracles. Out of finding my security in Him I was later able to start connecting back to the Body, although the Body seemed paralyzed by the shocking event in my life when it should have reached out towards me. I was able to forgive without being asked for forgiveness and I was able to love without expecting to be understood or even loved in return. But I did not look to make any of these things happen in me; what I looked for was survival; my only hope for life was Jesus and my encounter with Him empowered me to invest myself in the community because I have tasted the living waters and I was not thirsty any longer. I was able to feed others because I was being fed the living bread by Him.

My first prayer after Claudiu died – whilst he was still in the house, waiting for the police to come – was: "God, you know it is not the right time for me to stop living now, I am only 25. If I lose my next decade in depression, I might end up alone and on the street. I cannot afford not to be able to work. If You brought me to this point, You have to take me through it." I do not think I can express in words how I felt that short prayer impacted God's heart; but it felt like that prayer was an iron pin that connected my heart to God's because in that prayer my heart was stripped, completely open and naked, exposed and vulnerable. And God, who is always honest and completely open, without any shadow of duplicity, invaded it. From that point it felt as if I was dragged in a deep tornado, and the only thing I was able to do was to close my eyes, wrap myself around

Him, and allow Him to take me through it. Looking back, I realize even more the horrifying context I was in. Yet at the time, I did not even realize how dramatic everything was, although I literally had moments when I did not think that I would make it through – not necessarily because of my inner pain but because the entire context I was in, was unbelievable – spiritually, financially, relationship-wise. But this is what healing that comes from Him looks like, it starts like a small iron pin that pierces His heart for your pain; and somehow as the days pass by you realize that the iron pin has grown into an anchor that cannot be moved. It is that anchoring prayer that was an apparently insignificant act of devotion that kept me from sinking and gave me a foundation to build on. Anything else would have been a personal struggle and it would not have lasted.

After this first step of abandoning self in God's hand, the second one and all the subsequent steps were decided by the Holy Spirit in my life. Because of the complex circumstances I was in, I gave away and threw out everything that belonged to Claudiu, but remained in the same house for four more years, with various periods of two to three months living away. But God might not ask you to sell your house. There was nothing that I did after that encounter with Him that had such a great impact in my life and there was nothing that changed my life to such a degree as the choice to seek Jesus. After that, I did what He told me to do; there might be things that are wise to do because at the end of the day, we are all humans, but there will be particular things that He will ask you to do. He might ask you to sell your house or He might not. He might ask you to quit your job or He might not. He might ask you to start working if your spouse who provided for you has passed away. But no decision is to be taken unless the first step of encountering Him is made. That is true for both Christians and non-Christians. I was born and raised in a Christian family and I was baptized in water and in the Spirit when I was 15; but I needed a fresh encounter with Him, a new revelation for a new circumstance. I needed a new understanding of His friendship and redemptive love.

Do not do what the Bible clearly tells us not to do. Make it as simple as possible: a short prayer from the depth of your heart will do miracles. It is only between you and God. Silence any other voice.

HOW DO YOU KNOW WHEN YOU ARE HEALED?

I do not think that we always understand the impact that our own lack of healing has on the Body of Christ. Whatever is not healed on an emotional level causes a chain reaction of hurt in the Body, because it will cause us to be unable to love others and to react in an abnormal fashion to love. The church we are in might be the most loving one but if we have deep, unhealed wounds and we are not intentional in our relationship with Christ, continuously exposing our hearts to the point of emptying ourselves completely towards Him regardless of the cost, we will hinder the unity that the Holy Spirit works towards in the Body. The consequence of Hebrews 11 is spelled out in Hebrews 12:1-2:

"Therefore then, since we are surrounded by so great a cloud of witnesses [who have borne testimony to the Truth], let us strip off and throw aside every encumbrance (unnecessary weight) and that sin which so readily (deftly and cleverly) clings to and entangles us, and let us run with patient endurance and steady and active persistence the appointed course of the race that is set before us, looking away [from all that will distract] to Jesus, Who is the Leader and the Source of our faith [giving the first incentive for our belief] and is also its Finisher [bringing it to maturity and perfection]. He, for the joy [of obtaining the prize] that was set before Him, endured the cross, despising and ignoring the shame, and is now seated at the right hand of the throne of God."

I previously said that ignoring a broken leg does not mean that the break is undone, it just means that a serious trauma is ignored and when (not "if"!) the leg will be needed to walk on, it will hurt even more than at the time of the injury. We need our hearts to love again. Some of us might never love in a romantic fashion again, if that is what God decides for us, but we still have children, parents, friends and brothers that we need to be able to love and who need us to love them. If we cannot receive God's healing love, we will not be able to love others and if we cannot love others we will never be whole.

One of the first characteristics of a healed wound is that it has a scab and pus does not come out when it is squeezed. That is what a loving heart is like – it does not produce any more pus (bitterness, unforgiveness, anger); it produces the fruits of love listed in Galatians chapter 5: love, joy, peace, patience, kindness, goodness, faith, gentleness, self-control.

Another great proof is that looking back you can recognize God's hand in the midst of your darkest hour and you are grateful that He was with you, no matter how deep and dark the valley was. You remember His grip on your hand more than you remember the shadows.

Another proof of a healed heart is that out of your walk with God you can teach others not only about the pain you experienced, but about God's utterly steadfast character and unfailing, limitless love. You know things about Him that others do not know and you are eager to share them with others, to encourage them and to lift them. You become someone who can hold someone else's hand when they go through the same circumstances – and you do it without pointing to yourself but pointing towards God.

Another proof of a healed heart is that you no longer search for anything else to replace your loss. Once you have Him, you have everything you need. You will not look for a partner to be happy any more. God completely embarrassed me through a homosexual atheist who listened to me testifying about who God is. He told me: "*You know... if I believed God is who you say He is, I would never need anything else. I have no idea what you are looking for any more, if you found Him and He is like you say He is.*" That remark made me repent of my *you are not good enough for me, God* attitude; God became not only enough, but abundant in my heart.

Probably the ultimate proof of healing is that you no longer need happiness to be happy. Your happiness will no longer be based on being happy or being "like the rest of the world", but on being holy. When your happiness springs from your holiness you will know that you are not only healed but abundantly fruitful.

CHAPTER IV

THE LIE, THE TRUTH, THE DARE

THE LIE: YOU. AND YOU.

A great challenge for the Body of Christ is to move on from receiving information from the pulpit to applying what it already knows. If we would apply everything we know, our churches would be empty and we would be out there making disciples. We need to apply what we know.

As children of our Father we need to be intentional in moving from receiving revelation to allowing the Spirit to implement in our lives the truth and the life it carries. This means that sometimes we need to go the extra mile and ask ourselves what exactly the Word that is spoken over us means in the reality of our earthly lives. If we decide to do so, how can we internalize God's word? This makes the difference between having information and actually living out the Truth.

After understanding that God is constant, we have to take a step further and understand how God operates through His Spirit and how the devil destroys His work. These all seem to be unrelated to the issue of pain, but when we are in hard places, the last thing we have time to do is work out what we believe. We have to be prepared to face the storm before it hits. It is never too soon to be ready. In pain and struggle it is not only much less efficient to try to untangle all the questions that are bubbling up in our minds, but it can also be dangerous because at that point, we would cling on to any voice that offers what we believe we need in order to be able to get out of that painful place. If we do not know how to differentiate the voice of the Shepherd from the voice of the enemy we are literally lost. The place where anyone would want to be absolutely sure they walk with God, following God's voice is in the sandstorm – when we cannot even keep our eyes open.

We are workers together with God, which actually means that He is glorified now in us by our willingness to allow Him to bring forth His Kingdom on earth through us. We are His helpers; we help Him bring into life what God speaks because the Spirit is in us. We cannot do anything disconnected from Him, so the ability to bring into our kingdom His Kingdom is not ours; it is still His. We are co-operating with God, being led and taken over by the Spirit, to create out of nothing the Kingdom. The example that Christ set for us is that He submitted completely, to the point of death, to the will of the Father, and He was the first one who actively engaged in bringing the Kingdom of God into being. He is the Cornerstone, the first one who actually broke through the curse of this earth by bringing forth the massive work of pulling down God's authority onto the earth as it is in Heaven. Jesus broke the curse, and after the initial crack He made in the canopy of sin that enfolds this sad planet, the disciples followed His example and spread across the Earth, taking the Kingdom wherever their feet touched the land.

The way God created is called *ex-nihilo* i.e. out of nothing. I remember hearing in the first days of my widowhood about *ex-nihilo* creation, which means that God, and no other being, does not create from preexisting blocks of matter, but He actually creates matter; creation was deliberately made by God as a supernatural act; it is a proof of His majesty.

The implication of the ex-nihilo creation belonging only to God is greater than we might first understand. The consequence of His uniqueness in the way He creates is that whatever the devil does is not original. He portrays himself as being as big as God, constantly troubling God and constantly wresting control from Him. In fact, there are major religious movements that are based on the equality between good and evil. It is not true. It is not at all like that! The devil can only misuse what God has already created. God knows the measure of the enemy's power and He is not allowing the enemy to strike us harder than we can fight back. That is actually what the Bible tells us in Isaiah chapter 54 verse 17:

"No weapon forged against you will prevail, and you will refute every tongue that accuses you. This is the heritage of the servants of the Lord, and this is their vindication from me," declares the Lord."

The only way the devil can try to trick us is not by creating something new, but by following what God is doing on earth as He brings down His Kingdom, and make it seem less or more or slightly different than what it actually is. In other words, the devil's work never precedes in time the work of the Holy Spirit. It comes after and alters it, but it comes out of his attentive observation of the way the Spirit moves. The Spirit of God creates ex-nihilo and the devil spoils it, and then tells us it was all God's idea – remember the temptation in Eden? Remember Jesus temptation? Both temptations boil down to the misusing and the misinterpreting of the Word of God.

The Bride has the responsibility to move closer towards her Groom, regardless.

During my very early years I lived in communist Romania, in which the control of the party went almost as far as it is described in George Orwell's "1984". The spiritual battle meant standing against a spirit which tried to level down the healthy personal image of self, by trying to develop a mass-mentality of "I don't matter" and an extreme lack of "persona". To illustrate how far this was taken, the flats were designed in a way that regardless how people would shift the standard-sized furniture around in the room, they would not have more space than their neighbor. When politics actively influences architecture and design to such a degree, it means that the ideology is rooted so deep in the society that it will take a miracle to get rid of it. And this is exactly what the redemptive hand of the Spirit in the age of socialism had to restore: it had to restore the Bride's perception of how God was seeing us: as *united in our diversity*, not as identical and divided. It had to break off the yoke of believing we lack value. In the age when there was always a political or religious power that rose to control the entire society by means of imposing a forced unity under a banner of belonging to a party or a movement, the need for the Spirit to tell us that God loves us as individuals and that we are not bound by the flesh was vital. The work of the Spirit in that age was to make room in our hearts for a personal relationship with the Son of God, but the emphasis was never on us and it will never be; the Spirit *always* points towards the Cross, it always speaks about Him, about the Son of God. In other words, emphasis of the Spirit, even in a socialist system, *"Who is JESUS for you?"* not *"Who is Jesus for YOU?"*. Yet we misinterpreted His words of encouragement to develop as individuals, and we reached the conclusion that we are so important that we must be pursued by God merely because *He* is dependent on making us happy.

The truth is, in a totalitarian system, which is by definition abusive and allows no awareness of a *personal* relationship with God (or as a matter of fact, with anyone) because there is no notion of what being a *person* really entails, it was vital that for the Holy Spirit to teach the Bride about the uniqueness of each person. Under the communist system in Romania, the idea of equality and homogeneity and lack of personal importance among individuals got to the point where the design of apartment buildings was standardized to the maximum. The doors, the rooms, the bathrooms were all a standard size, etc. The furniture, as well, was all the same size. Everything was standardized. All traditional crafts and personalized sizes for furniture or apartments were virtually done away with. The result was that no matter how the furniture was placed around the room, the free space remained in the room was exactly the same as the neighbor's. That is diabolical. In that culture the Spirit needed to tell the Bride: "You are important. You are unique. I love you." People needed to hear that they have worth and that they are important to the Lord Jesus Christ not only corporately, and not only as robots that can produce x pairs of socks in y minutes. And we still need to know and hear that God loves us, each of us, personally – we do not have to forget that hard-learned lesson. Widows still need to learn that God is their protector when they feel abandoned and exposed; sick people to hear that God is their healer. Orphans need to learn that God is their Father when they have no one to run to. Foreigners need to learn to trust Him as their friend when the phone does not ring for months and months. Keeping that in mind, we also need to understand that the devil cannot speak words that human beings could live on. Mathew 4:4 says:

"But He replied, It has been written, Man shall not live and be upheld and sustained by bread alone, but by every word that comes forth from the mouth of God."

So the words that *created* and *maintain* life belong to God. Hence one of the devil's works is to take what God says, the *living* word, use it in the wrong context, and feed it to the world. He cannot speak words that carry life in them for us to be spiritually fed by them (by believing them!) – so he misquotes God's words and feeds it to us.

The direction of the culture of the world comes after the revelation that the Spirit brings to the Bide; it is always the "devil's translation" of the Word of God for humanity. We all know that pushing a truth further than it was originally intended to extend, distort and falsify it.

The only reason why it sometimes seems that it is the worldly culture leading the church and not the church leading the culture, is because sadly, it is exactly so! And it is not God's fault, nor His intention! Whenever we become lazy in spirit and listen to the lies that the devil tells us while the Spirit tries to cover the noisy lying voices that we listen to, we create the opportunity for the adversary to steal the Word, *"translate"* it to us and present it as God's word. The evil one actually is more interested in and more attentive to what our Father is doing and saying than we are, and we are allowing him to take the perfect word of God and muddy it by subtly changing it; but of course, the life that the Word carries within it is still active, just as the Word of God was active in the Garden of Eden when the consequences of God's words happened exactly as He originally spoke them, regardless of what the devil's interpretation of them was! The Bride is too relaxed in a self-protective, defensive attitude towards culture; she only reacts to culture with a constant amazement of *"what this world believes lately"*, without being prepared for what is coming in the future because we, the ones who are His Bride, are SO focused on ourselves and on our pain that we forget that it is NOT about us, it is about Jesus! How sad is that? If we actually wanted to hear God's Words as He speaks them, understand that they *really* create exactly as they are spoken, act upon them through the power of the Holy Spirit *immediately* and *before* the devil takes them and alters them, even pain would be eradicated because God's plan of bringing the Kingdom down to earth implies abolition of pain! It implies binding the devil and exposing all his lies!

In other words, we tend to do it all in the wrong order - our focus should *not* be on *us* and the fulfillment of our desires in our relationship with Jesus, but the fulfillment of His will and His plan in relationship with us; and when His spoken will becomes reality, it is then that our healing takes place. Healing is a *constant* consequence of His *constantly* good and perfect will, not an isolated selfish target that someone needs to convince Him to perform. We do not have to convince God to be good, He really is good – it is just that we do not know what *good* means!

So the issue that actually stands in the way of our healing is that since the Word has been perverted by the devil, we have developed our own democratic views and our individual approaches on *every* and *any* topic, and we have moved far away from what God said about His perspective on people. We have crossed the fine line that separates individuality from individualism by believing that WE are the ones glorified by our personal relationship with Christ, not Him. When Christ speaks about His love for us, it is not "My love is for *you*!", it is "*My* love is for you." And this leads to one stronghold that we need to take down in our lives: if we emphasize only one characteristic of God because that is what *we* need Him to be at that particular time or circumstance, and we believe that one of His attributes defines Him fully, we fall into the trap of creating an idol. God is a God of rest, but if we only preach and teach rest, we develop a lazy Body. God does rest, but He also works. God is a God of resurrection and He is a God of healing, but He is a God who decided to give us free will, which implies bearing as moral beings the consequences of our choices. God is a God of uniqueness. He decides when to act in your life with healing; He decides when to act in your loved one's life with resurrection. He decides when not to. Who are we to hold Him accountable?

So maybe the right question in post-modernism, when we are very much aware (*too much?*) of ourselves, is not "Who is Jesus *for you?*". In a sense, we have already blunted the edge of that question by twisting what the Spirit told the Bride about the importance of each individual, thinking that if God is looking for each of us individually, the entire story is about *us* – when in fact, it is about *Him.* Maybe the right question to ask now is "Who is *Jesus?*", or "*Who does the Bible say that Jesus is?*"

We have to stop defining Jesus in relation to us, and define us in relation to Him. We have to understand that unless we gain the Father's perspective, we fail to see who Jesus is. God's eyes see the truth; our eyes have a self-oriented and limited view.

THE TRUTH: LIKE A ROOT OUT OF DRY GROUND

This is what God the Father says about Jesus, the Son, in Isaiah 53:

"For [the Servant of God] grew up before Him like a tender plant, and like a root out of dry ground; He has no form or comeliness [royal, kingly pomp], that we should look at Him, and no beauty that we should desire Him.

He was despised and rejected and forsaken by men, a Man of sorrows and pains, and acquainted with grief and sickness; and like One from Whom men hide their faces He was despised, and we did not appreciate His worth or have any esteem for Him.

Surely He has borne our grief (sicknesses, weaknesses, and distresses) and carried our sorrows and pains [of punishment], yet we [ignorantly] considered Him stricken, smitten, and afflicted by God [as if with leprosy].

But He was wounded for our transgressions, He was bruised for our guilt and iniquities; the chastisement [needful to obtain] peace and well-being for us was upon Him, and with the stripes [that wounded] Him we are healed and made whole.

All we like sheep have gone astray, we have turned everyone to his own way; and the Lord has made to light upon Him the guilt and iniquity of us all.

He was oppressed, [yet when] He was afflicted, He was submissive and opened not His mouth; like a lamb that is led to the slaughter, and as a sheep before her shearers is dumb, so He opened not His mouth.

By oppression and judgment He was taken away; and as for His generation, who among them considered that He was cut off out of the land of the living [stricken to His death] for the transgression of my [Isaiah's] people, to whom the stroke was due?

And they assigned Him a grave with the wicked, and with a rich man in His death, although He had done no violence, neither was any deceit in His mouth.

Yet it was the will of the Lord to bruise Him; He has put Him to grief and made Him sick. When You and He make His life an offering for sin [and He has risen from the dead, in time to come], He shall see His [spiritual] offspring, He shall prolong His days, and the will and pleasure of the Lord shall prosper in His hand.

He shall see [the fruit] of the travail of His soul and be satisfied; by His knowledge of Himself [which He possesses and imparts to others] shall My [uncompromisingly] righteous One, My Servant, justify many and make many righteous (upright and in right standing with God), for He shall bear their iniquities and their guilt [with the consequences, says the Lord].

Therefore will I divide Him a portion with the great [kings and rulers], and He shall divide the spoil with the mighty, because He poured out His life unto death, and [He let Himself] be regarded as a criminal and be numbered with the transgressors; yet He bore [and took away] the sin of many and made intercession for the transgressors (the rebellious)."

Jesus did not ask anyone and did not seek to receive permission from anyone to be right with God. His relationship with God did not depend on the acceptance of society, on the way He was accepted by the culture of His day, or on His marital status. In fact, after the fall, there was simply no possibility for any human to be in right standing before God, which is exactly why the Law was sent: to prove that our efforts, no matter how great they are, are futile and meaningless. Jesus stood no chance of living a life pleasing to God, if He had not abandoned Himself to the Holy Spirit and fed on God's Words daily. Jonathan Edwards, the great theologian, speaks about the concept of *vital connection* with God. It is the most accurate way of referring to the relationship Jesus had with God. Jesus was the first man to live out completely a relationship with God that broke the curse because it continuously went against it until the curse (brought about by the Fall) was broken off.

The divinity of Christ is reflected in His humanity, not denied by it. The *human* that was *born from God* is the *only kind of human* that can be the image and likeness of God. In this sense, the Lord Jesus Christ is:

- vitally connected to God, regardless of the context or the consequences
- completely abandoned to God's will, again regardless of the context or the consequences
- in a personal relationship with the Father, again regardless of the context or the consequences
- not dependent on any human, again regardless of the context or the consequences

Jesus couldn't feed Himself with the words of the teachers of the law, because these words were impure. He couldn't be taught by them because they were not teaching the Law, they were teaching the tradition. There was no filling with the Holy Spirit until He came. He was the First to be filled with the Spirit. There was nothing this world contributed to enable Him to be who He was. In other words, He did not come to play any role, whether that of healer, or prophet, or miraculous bread maker. And when Pilate asked Him to perform a miracle, or when He was nailed to the Cross and the priests mocked Him because He made no attempt to save Himself from death and pain, it was not because He lost His ability to do any of these things, but because His presence there meant bringing the Kingdom down, not doing what people randomly asked out of curiosity or despair or naivety. Since He is constant, He will not produce today miracles to gratify our flesh. He is in our lives exactly who He is, not who we want Him to be. We are not the ones who define His role in our lives; neither do our needs nor our human capacities (flesh) define Him.

And yes, today Jesus IS resurrected, He IS alive, He IS healed of all the physical, emotional and psychological abuse He suffered on the Cross. But His resurrection, His bringing back to life, His healing, did not depend on anyone or anything else than His relationship with the Father. His life did not depend on the context He was born in – He was born in *dry ground.* There is no plant that can grow out of dry ground! Have you ever seen dry ground? It is lifeless! Life does not spring out of it! Yet, that is where Jesus was born and His relationship with the Father was far more intense than the context He was born into. It was stronger than death, and it defeated death. It was so intense that it had the power to overcome the natural and defeat the law of growth. God grew Jesus in relationship with Him, through the power of the Holy Spirit, for His plan and purpose. The truth is, when someone does not depend on anyone, he is who he is. – Is that not our Lord's name? **"I AM WHO I AM."**

Because we are affected by sin, we sometimes have wrong expectations of God, of those around us, of our partners and of ourselves. The only realistic expectation that we can have of anyone is that we all have to face the reality of being in a *personal* relationship with God, and that this relationship is vital to *us*, not to God. He is who He is; we are to be who we are, *in Him.*

An overwhelming percentage of the pain that widows experience is caused by the wrong expectations we have of God. The more we allow the devil to distort the image we have of God, the more we will have unrealistic expectations, the more we will replace God with an idol and the more we will suffer. That is why it is so important to pay attention to what the Bible teaches us about Jesus and what He shows us about our Lord. Knowing Jesus means knowing the Lord we serve, and it also means knowing what we are supposed to be doing, and includes knowing the Father.

THE DARE: CHRIST IN YOU, YOU IN CHRIST

If we know who He is, we know who we are. If we know who we are, we will relate in a healthy and biblical way to our family. We will not make idols of our families and we will not refashion God according to our need. But the more we are deceived, the more unclear the view on the issue of marriage is in a society and the greater the depression of the unmarried and the greater the struggle of the recovering widows is. People that have a healthy teaching on marriage have an easier time recovering after their partner is no longer with them. I realized a great percentage of my "Oh my God, what do I do now?" moments as a widow were caused by a wrong mental and emotional setting generated by my unrealistic perception of external factors. It took me a lot of time to pray and meditate on God's Word to be able to discern which aspects of my education were genuinely biblical and which were parts of "folk wisdom". Having the Bible at hand is a privilege so many generations have not had! We can so easily understand who God is nowadays, because we have the Bible and we have the Spirit. David had neither, and he still managed to be a man after God's heart!

Among our friends, Claudiu and I were the first ones to get married. We did not receive any marriage preparation or counseling nor indeed any advice from friends because when we got married, no close friend knew anything more than we did, and sadly, during that time in our lives we were both part of very bashful churches, hence our pastors did not even consider the idea of premarital counseling. And sadly, the community's main issue prior to our getting married was: "Are you still both virgins? If yes, why? If no, why?" and few days after we were married people started asking about babies, as if when the wedding is over, you tick a box on a list and then you move on to the next point. Part of the issue is that – for some odd reason – we, humans, believe life has a pattern and if someone does not fit that predefined pattern, there must be something wrong with that person. When it comes to marriage, that puts a lot of pressure on the ones that are different to what we find as "normal": the single, the divorced, the widows and those that cannot have children. On all of these people, not only the society but the church as well places considerable pressure. It is an unjustified expectation though, since most these people belong to groupings that they have not chosen to belong to.

These are some common misconceptions – based on the devil's lies and human weakness – that severely hit most of the people in their 30's that I knew, especially women and widows. I am sharing these thoughts because I believe we need to take a stand against these lies and their effects on us before we even consider marrying in the first place. We need to make them clear throughout Christian media and in our Churches. No one wants to see their children orphans or widows, but if they end up in that place, misguided, albeit well-meaning teaching on the topic of marriage will have severe consequences.

After Claudiu died, I had to seriously reevaluate what I believed marriage, singlehood and widowhood were. This process was triggered because I was left completely alone when he died and I had to decide myself if I wanted to be healed or not and if I wanted my pain to be used by God to His glory or not because there was no parent, no child, no friend to save me from falling into self-pity. His death brought out the worst both in the people around me and in me, and the only person I have been able and entitled to deal with was my very own self. I had to deal with myself first in order to be able to deal with others as soon as possible, as some of them would have swallowed me alive now that I was defenseless. I had to "woman-up" and deal with it. While doing that, I realized that I grew up having wrong ideas about marriage and I continued believing them as a young wife and the potential of being crushed when I became widowed was not in what was happening around me, although it was messy and bloody, but in what I believed about myself and about God. I do not even want to imagine where I would have ended up if the Spirit of God had not opened my eyes to see the lies and prompted me to break out of the bondage. But God was good and gracious with me! My diaries and my private blogs contain uncountable prayers and proofs of my inner struggles followed by priceless songs of thanksgiving to my Lord for His deliverance.

UNCOVERING THE LIES

The following lies are the ones I realized I was struggling to pin-point in my life. I have seen the enemy using them in the lives of others as well, as they were going through the valley of the shadow of death. The reason why I am sharing them is because if we are aware of the enemy's schemes, we can overcome them easier.

THE "ONLY MARRIAGE BRINGS HAPPINES" LIE

One of my favorite authors – the dearest one – is the controversial Clive Staples Lewis. He asks in "The Problem of Pain" (1940) "Is not God supposed to be good? Is not God supposed to love us? And does God want us to suffer? What if the answer to that question is yes? Because I am not sure that God particularly wants us to be happy. I think He wants us to be able to love and be loved. He wants us to grow up. I suggest to you that it is because God loves us that He makes us the gift of suffering."

Although people get married with the hope their spouse will make them happy (and they divorce because their spouse fails to make them happy), I am not sure myself that the purpose of life or the purpose of a marriage is to be happy. I believe it is growing in likeness with Jesus. It is growing in holiness. Happiness is a consequence of being in a relationship with God. But we are unable to be in a relationship with God unless we are holy. God cannot stand sin and sin cannot stand in the presence of God. Hence, happiness is a consequence of being holy.

Marriage is not about "How can that person make me happy?", it is about two persons strongly anchored in God working together in perfect unity and moving together in the greatest degree of intimacy towards God. But the move is towards God. True unity in a couple's relationship is a consequence of each individual's relationship with God. It is their unity as a couple that stands on their individual relationship with Christ, not their relationship with Christ standing on their unity as a couple. Personalities, characters and individuality are not allowed to be absorbed in another person's identity, but in Christ.

Have you met persons that have been through horrid experiences in their life? Have you met persons that carry deadly illnesses in their bodies and yet are still smiling and worshiping the Lord? I have. They are the happiest people on his earth. They have amazing insights about God. They love Him and He loves them. I have met rich people, influential people, married and with children; some of them were the saddest I have ever met. Because nothing and no one other than Jesus brings sufficiency to the level where we are happy about who we are. A marriage does not do that by simply changing our marital status. A marriage is, in essence, an oath between two sinners, which, unless they willingly go through the process of being sanctified and become happy as a consequence of their continuous sanctification, will make each other's lives miserable. And the widowed need to be reminded of this – and as widows, we should not forget that. Because if we believe the key to happiness is marriage, as soon as our partner dies we will run out and marry the first remotely suitable person we meet. No! Do not do it! We need to seek out Jesus; we need to get a stronger grip on Him. He is our source of happiness. Unless we are in Him and He is in us, married or unmarried or widowed or divorced, we are equally unhappy. And we have the surprising ability to make ourselves increasingly unhappy if we seek happiness in the wrong place and for the wrong reasons. No one should marry *solely* to be happy – that is selfishness. Especially widows that have experienced deep hurt in the past should not on any account, rush into marriage thinking: "I was happy when I was married, now I am unmarried and I am unhappy. Solution: marry." No! Most times the reason why we were happy when we were married and we are unhappy in widowhood is because our partner did his best and we were blessed by God. But when our spouse dies, we are not stepping out of God's blessing. He is still concerned about us, about our sanctification, and He still blesses us. But if we blame God and we are building a wall between us and Him, we are the ones who step away from His presence and blessing, not God the One who moves away from us.

The presence of a partner in our life is a blessing, not a vital necessity without which we can never be happy (or happy again). The *only* vital necessity any human has is his relationship with Jesus – I cannot emphasize it enough. Nothing but Jesus and Jesus alone is the answer to whatever the question is.

It is true that there are people that have a deeper need of companionship, and there is nothing wrong with that as long as this need does not grow deeper than the need for God. There is nothing wrong with the desire to have a family, there is nothing wrong with feeling the pain of the absence of a partner or missing our spouse. We are created to have relationships; we are created to long to be with someone. We are created to have intimacy with another human being and God Himself decided that it is not good for us to be alone, but we are *not* created to find our happiness in anything other than Jesus. One of the most brutally honest passages I came across is from St. Augustine's Confessions (another loved author) where he states: "You have made us for yourself, O Lord, and our heart is restless until it rests in You."

When we are absolutely convinced that we cannot be happy without being married or in a relationship, when the devil can convince us of that, he has won. We will blame God for taking away our happiness (when in fact we are looking for happiness in the wrong place); and we will take matters into our own hands and we will do anything to be happy again, to grasp the thing that we think will satisfy our deeper need. And if we cannot snatch a partner from God's hands, we will use any available way we have to get one: if we have to, we will even split up a family – let's not pretend that this is not happening in our churches as well as in the world... We underestimate the drive, the hunger and the determination of a raging heart dependent on its idol. The drive is supernatural because we were created to have the supernatural need for God. After all, we are *spiritual* beings. If we direct this hunger towards something else, the intensity of it and drive are still there, even though they are misdirected.

I have come across many situations in which Christian widows convinced they could not be happy if they did not remarry, got involved with married persons in the hope of eventually having them for good. The consequences were devastating in every single instance like this. Families have break up, and children grow up fatherless, God's name was taken in vain, neighbors saw and talked about it and our God was mocked.

The only relationship from which we are created to extract our happiness is the relationship that we have with Jesus. Jesus is our fuel, and we *can*, like Him, grow *like a root out of dry land* if we extract our life from Him, rather than from circumstances. That is why we eat His Body and we drink His Blood when we have communion. We are rooted in Him, not in our marital status.

If being married is to us more important than being holy, we are idolaters. Marriage worshipers are not Jesus worshipers.

THE "HALF-MAN" LIE

I believe this is the lie that I have come across the most often, in Christian as well as in non-believers circles. The way this lie is told is usually really candid – we do not even think what these expressions imply: "my better half", "Have you found your other half yet?", "When your half comes along …", "You complete me."

Of course, expressing the depths of the purest delight caused by the existence of our partner by our side is not a bad thing; but I started really listening to what these expressions actually mean when I was struggling to get back on my feet. And I realized that these expressions actually suggest – figuratively speaking - that I, as a widow, only have one foot left, only one arm left, maybe one kidney and certainly only half a heart since I had shared mine with my partner. Hurting and trying to get back on my feet, I had to react quickly to the reality around me, for otherwise I would have been buried under piles of unpaid bills, bank loans, etc. and I realized this was one of the lies that had a great impact on my life. I realized that I did not trust God to take care of *me* and the financial aspect of *my* life in any other way than through a husband whom I suddenly no longer had. I did not see God looking at *me* as an *individual*, I perceived Him perceiving Claudiu and myself as one being, one identity. Of course, in the sense of unity and oneness in family, it is true that we were one, but me, *Ligia*, did not disappear once my husband died. With my husband alive or dead, I was still a fully developed adult that needed not only to be able to take care of herself but also to have a heart of compassion for others and serve the new-born in Christ within the community. This is actually the key to what the Apostle Paul says in 1 Timothy 5 about women who are qualified to be treated as widows. You cannot expect a person who has lost a leg to be able to run. If we teach the young generation that *marriage* is what makes a person a fully functional and complete being, as opposed to teaching them how the new-birth will not leave them lacking anything, we basically prepare our young for the message of the world who is quick to offer them surrogates for the halves they miss. Can you see how the enemy makes the most out of our lack of vigilance?

Nowhere in the Bible have I found the expression *the other half of this or that person*. What we find about married people and their relationship with God is that God always treats the spouses in a way that emphasizes the need for both of them to develop a personal relationship with Him. He sees the man in relation with Him and He sees the woman in relation with Him. This is the foundation of a healthy family: both partners are supposed to have and cultivate a healthy, personal relationship with Jesus. It is only if you stand on both feet that when the storm comes you do not fall. Imagine trying to navigate through a storm standing in one foot: impossible.

I love how the Bible emphasizes the relationship God has with both partners. If we look at Adam and Eve, God does not call them in the Garden "Family X, what have you done?" – He asks them to answer about their sins individually, although both Adam and Eve have the tendency to get a third party involved in this two-person dialogue – Adam blames Eve, Eve blames the snake (probably because there was no one else left to blame).

The example of Nabal and Abigail (1 Samuel 25) is also relevant when it comes to how God deals with couples: Nabal did not listen to David's plea and was eventually killed by God, but Abigail reacted against her husband's folly and the Lord kept her alive and blessed her. God cares about people and cares about their destiny in particular. He knows us by name, and when we make our marriage vows we are neither supposed to "melt" into our partner's personality nor to lose awareness of who we are as individuals. Both partners willingly and maturely go down the same path in life but they are always two people traveling road, not a four-eyed being. Partners should always keep their individual identity as they are in complete agreement about God's plan for their life as a family. One plus one does not equal one when it comes to stand before God.

The Scripture exhorts us many times to *be one* with the partner as the Father, the Son and the Holy Ghost are one in nature, so the best illustration of the oneness that the Bible gives for the family is the illustration of the Trinity: three distinct persons sharing the same nature. The Father is never mistaken either for the Son or for the Holy Spirit. They are one in their plans and in their goals, in nature and desires, but God the Father did not die on the Cross. It is God the Son who came as a human being and died on the cross for us. We do not believe in one God that wears three masks, we believe in a Triune God. Likewise, we do not believe in a one-person marriage, we believe in a bi-one marriage.

Even in cases where both partners had the same fate because they shared the same heart – like Ananias and Sapphira – they still both had individual responsibility for their actions. If we do not understand how serious God is about each person keeping their own identity and how He relates to us first as individuals, we will easily fall when our partners die because we will feel as if we were split in half. It might not seem important to underline the importance of the personal relationship with Christ, but if we do not understand it, even without realizing we might end up believing that our salvation depends on our partner as well, since our personalities merge into each other. But our relationship with Christ does not depend on our marriage partner, just as our happiness does not. Our salvation depends on how the issue of sin and consequently, holiness, is managed: our sins will be paid either by the blood of Jesus or our own blood. The partner has no right of veto in this regard, even in he/she wanted to.

When talking about His coming, Jesus gives the disciples the example of Lot and his wife, another couple in which God's personal relationship with both partners is revealed (Luke 17:32-35):

"Remember Lot's wife! Whoever tries to keep their life will lose it, and whoever loses their life will preserve it. I tell you, on that night two people will be in one bed; one will be taken and the other left. Two women will be grinding grain together; one will be taken and the other left."

Do not allow the devil to tell you that when you became widowed, half of you died. That is not true. You do not need another person in order to be complete, although being ripped away from the person with whom you grew in unity for many years might be the most painful experience you go through. But that is not the end of *you*, it is the end of your marriage. You did not break apart; nothing of what you are is missing. And that is one of the greatest gifts that God ever bestowed upon humanity: the capacity to maintain our own identity in a unifying relationship like marriage. It is not a punishment that we cannot be absorbed into one another, it is a blessing. In fact, psychologists call dysfunctional marriages, those in which one or both of the partners get sucked into a *codependent relationship*. Co-dependent relationships are damaging even without the trauma of widowhood. Widowhood and death only bring to the surface the wrong soul-tie created in such a marriage. We were not created to live in codependent relationships whether with the living or the dead. We were created to only be *in Christ*, not *in our spouses*, spiritually speaking.

There's another reason why I find understanding this truth crucial; it is because if God in His grace decides that we are more effective as singles (prior to getting married or after being widowed), unless we understand this truth and live in the freedom it brings, we tend to feel as if there's a void that needs to be filled by a person and we will not bear fruit because we are not aware that we have everything we need to bear fruit. Even though we are fully able to be fruitful after our partner dies, we will be lied to by the devil that we cannot and we will be tempted to believe him. That is why so many single people that are in the Church, who are fully equipped Christians do not go to war: the devil lies that they lack what they need to go to war and they naively believe it.

The devil's plan is to neutralize Christians – and sometimes his lies make no sense - yet Christians still believe him! When the Spirit of God tells us to move and go forth, he will come up with excuses like: "Yes, but you are alone now. You are widowed." – How is that relevant to moving if we have both feet and we know we can move? It is only a good justification not to move if we previously believed we are only half a person unless we are married!

Do not mistake a blessing with a *must have* when it comes to our spiritual beings. We only *need* Jesus to be whole beings on earth. A partner is a so-much-needed blessing and God is the One Who decides what blessings He gives and when to grant them in our lives. But a partner is not *vital* for our existence.

Related to unveiling the dangers of believing this lie, I would also like to make a comment about the over-romantic cultural products and messages that we allow to penetrate our hearts. Women in particular are inclined to dream of a romantic love, and the desire in itself might as well be pure, not sinful. But when we make a purpose out of reading romantic literature or listen to love songs that send the wrong message about love and relationships, these might be factors that only deepen our pain and open old wounds. Be careful what you read; be careful what you listen to. Be careful what you feed your heart with. Read the Scriptures, not the kind of novels that make your heart yearn for a romantic love-story. A vulnerable heart is much easier to trick into bad relationships (adultery, homosexuality, sex outside marriage, etc.) than a healthy and alert heart. Do not feed your heart food that will weaken it. Be kind to yourself, but not indulgent. There is a big gap between kindness to self or self-indulgence. The former is rooted in grace, the latter in temptation. The former will produce the fruit of healing, the latter sin.

We do not bury half of ourselves when we bury a loved one; we just bury a person that we were placed *alongside* but not *inside*. We are placed *in Christ*, not *in the partner*. *In us* there is Christ, not our partner.

THE "LESSER I" LIE

This lie is another form of the previous lie. When a person gets married, it is obvious that the productivity of the couple grows in certain areas. Two people obviously have the potential to bear more fruit. Two people can clearly have greater financial power. Two people mean twice the power of one, if not even more. This is one of the reasons why God gave Eve to Adam: to grow his productivity. What that does not mean is that Adam would have been completely unproductive if Eve had never been created. Jesus was single His entire life. C.S. Lewis was single almost his entire life. The Apostle Paul was single. Mary, the mother of Jesus, was single when she found herself pregnant with the Son of God and her heart was submitted to the will of God in her singlehood.

When one partner dies, the other might feel as if s/he's half of what s/he was before because the amount of fruit that s/he bears is what one person can produce. This does not mean s/he is less than another person, it just means that the season of carrying the basket together with her/his partner is over, and now s/he has to bring the fruit of her/his life to Jesus alone, the quantity produced depending on the strength of her/his faith.

I believe the best example for this lie is when a man dies and his wife tries to be a mother and a father too: God *never* asks or intends that for her. God never expects a woman to become the father of her children, nor does He expect a man to become the mother of his children in addition to his original role in the family. God did not say: "*And if the father dies, the mother has to be a father too. That should fix everything.*" On the contrary, David says in Psalm 68:4, 5:

"*Sing to God, sing praises to His name, cast up a highway for Him Who rides through the deserts — His name is the Lord — be in high spirits and glory before Him! A father of the fatherless and a judge and protector of the widows is God in His holy habitation.*"

We are not called to take the place of the one who died; it is God's responsibility to do that. And He is the only one that can do it, without harming anyone in the process. We are not supposed to be the *joker* in the pack that can replace any other but has no intrinsic value. We still have a specific call and role in the family; and that does not include taking God's place. The place left free is not ours, but God's. The only way we can take this place is by pushing God aside – but do we really want to do that? Is that really wise? Do you really want, in the midst of the painful experience of losing a parent, your children to be robbed of the blessing of having God taking the place of the parent who died? God being a father to the fatherless is what makes the difference between being a part of God's family or not. He brings hope where there is no hope. If we rob our children of that experience, how will they know that God is the Father of the fatherless?

Do not feel as if you are less if you only do your part. You are not less; it is just fewer people carrying a load. The load will, obviously, decrease because God is good and gracious and He does not want us to be crushed under it so He steps in and carries the burden with us – if we allow Him to. Carrying what a single person carries is not a proof that a person is getting weaker, but merely shows that s/he is single.

Do not take upon yourself the task of being who you are not. Do not be a mother, if your children's mother has died. Do not let anyone tell you that you should be their mother. God loves them and even though a mother forgets her children, He does not. Would He ever forget your beloved children, if their mother has died? He will not. But you need to let Him shine through the painful storm. Trust Him. No one says your children will not hurt because they will and there is nothing you can do to prevent that; but they will hurt even if you do try to take on your spouse's load. They will hurt even more because in your struggling to keep balance, you will either push them away or crumble under the burden of widowhood, pain and confusion of who you are. Keep being who you were called to be and let God be Who He is. Allow Him to give meaning to your children's pain. God will not stay silent, He will fight for them. But if you keep pushing Him away by misunderstanding your call, you will make it even harder for your children to go through the whole experience. He will not fail you or your children; I grew up as an orphan, I became a widow and I lived as a foreigner in a country where I did not belong and had no friends. And I am testifying for Him, He has never failed me.

Not all people get married and not all of them stay married. Some of them decide they are more productive or fruitful as singles and stay so, others get divorced and others become widows. These statuses are ALL valid, if they are in Christ. No marital status should influence our capacity or willingness to bear fruit, even if society puts a lot of pressure on us to marry and have children. This is as unjust as discrimination based on race or gender. And it is harmful. Statistically, there are more singletons, divorcees and widows than married people. Although marriage and family are to be pursued, the ultimate goal is not a particular marital status but a holy lifestyle. A fruitful life is dependent solely on the relationship we have with our Lord. You are not less or more if you are widowed. You have the same responsibilities towards the Lord and the same position in Christ.

If losing your loved one makes you feel less than who Jesus says you are, the one whose words you internalized and the one who defined your identity is not Christ, but the one who died.

THE "GET IT OUT OF YOUR SYSTEM" LIE

This is one of the most convenient lies because it enables our flesh to manifest in the midst of our pain, thinking that if we have the excuse of hurting we can do whatever we want as we get immunity from condemnation brought about by sin; we might think God cannot condemn us because He is the One Who caused us pain in the first place.

The Truth is that there are no excuses for sin. There are no excuses to fall into the trap of addiction, self-medication, self-abuse, abuse of others, adultery, etc.

Healing does not come by running away from God. Forgiveness does not come by running away from Him. Peace does not come by running away from Him. Our dependency on God, the power of the bond between us and Him must be what determines our actions and reactions. Pain? The remedy is Jesus. Death? – Jesus. Deception? Failure? Confusion? Injustice? – JESUS. He is the answer to all of these.

He brings healing because He does not make us go into a numb state of unawareness. He does not have the effect of substances that make us forget the issue. He actually deals with the problem, He declares His victory over the circumstance and He gets us out of the mess. He *really* cares, and since He is a person, He understands our walk and He knows how to make sense of our affliction.

Whoever points you towards any solution other than Jesus, is misleading you. Motivational speeches are good. But they fade away after 5 minutes when the reality needs to be faced. Rather than hiding away, take heart and be courageous! Taking your pain to the cross is not easy, because there are things in your heart that He will point out as being displeasing to Him, and you will find yourself in the position of being hurt and afflicted and realizing that it is you who needs to repent of things you were not even aware you carry in your heart. It will not sound just, but it in fact it is God's mercy towards you that He does not allow pain to pass through you without cleansing you through it. So thank Him for His amazing care!

Part of being a Christian means that no matter what happens, you decide to stay at the cross with your heart exposed. Should a blazing fire burn your heart, you keep it exposed. Should waters feel like flooding your heart, you keep it exposed. You never cover it up, never put a protective cover over it, trusting that He will not allow anything to kill it, but He will measure and allow only as much as your heart can take. Not only will He allow no more than what it can take but He will use everything to cleanse it and produce fruit. If happiness is only present in your heart when things go according to your plan, there is not too much supernatural work going on in your heart.

You do not need to look for *creative ways* that allow you to flirt with sin to take away your pain. Go to Jesus. He knows exactly what your heart needs to be fruitful and to be healed. The message of the Bible is simple: "Come."

THE "SO MANY THINGS LEFT UNSAID..." LIE

The New International Translation of the Bible brings closer the meaning of this following Scripture that is familiar to many of us - Matthew 6, verses 25 to 34. Verse 27 rhetorically asks:

"Can any one of you by worrying add a single cubit to your height?" The recent translation brings the issue on an even more painful level: "Can any one of you by worrying add a single hour to your life?"

I haven't seen too many people being worried to tears about their height, but I have seen so many Christians being numbed after someone died because of the time they did not get to have with that person.

But having an extra hour with the one who passes away does not really make a difference when it comes to our understanding that we need to fix our eyes on Jesus in good times and bad. Having had the chance to do so, we would probably spend that hour doing something really human but really unwise – most likely begging God for a different ending, or making promises we cannot keep, or simply breaking our hearts in grief, not knowing what lies ahead.

The truth is, a lifetime lived in a particular way equals more than an hour of sharing thoughts in the panic of losing a person. The Bible tries to safeguard us through the Apostle Paul in Ephesians 4, where there is a general description of what the Christian life is supposed to look like. Many times we confuse the Bible's description of what our lives should look like after we are saved by grace with a list of things that we should do in order to become saved. It is true there are laws and commandments that the Bible is strict about, but considering the based-on-grace nature of the Gospel, the way passages like this one are supposed to be interpreted is not as a list of *do's* and *don'ts* but rather as descriptions of what our life should look like. God trusts the Spirit He has put in us to be sensitive and react when we discover that there is something in us that is not compatible with the description of what it the grace of God and the (finished) work of Jesus grace and Jesus's works (not our own deeds!) we are changed and begin to bear fruit.

This trap I find to be particularly dangerous, because I have seen the great effects it had in the life of someone who swallowed this lie. One of the widows I met was going through horrendous torment whenever she did not dream about her husband. Her family struggled for years to understand what made her so angry without any reason on random days; but what they did not know was that every morning when she woke up without having dreamed about her husband (who had passed away over three years earlier!) she would feel (in her own words) *"as if I cheated him; dirty and defiled. I am an unfaithful wife if I do not dream about him"*. Apparently, he (was it really him?) has been guiding her through her dreams every single night since he died. Of course, she idolized her husband to the point of worshiping him and by worshiping him she opened wide the door for encounters with other spirits. Idolatry does not only mean that we become absent from our relationship with Christ, it also means that we are present in a relationship with someone else and that we make ourselves available to have a personal relationship with another spirit. The memories that we have with the loved ones, when they are brought up to the surface or our hearts by the Holy Spirit, *never* make us doubt either His Sovereignty over the circumstance or His character; they *never* carry a directional message and they *never* disturb, vex, agitate or intrude on our adoration towards Christ. There is nothing that was left unsaid, there is nothing that needs to be said, and everything that was said, was supposed to be said. God really is in control of everything, and if He would have wanted you to have a particular conversation with the deceased one, He would have created the right context at the right timing for that conversation to take place. There is no reason, no reason at all, ever, we should look for guidance from the dead, speak to them or pray to them or feel guilty if we do not dream about them. All spiritual activity that you will find approved and encouraged in the Bible is worship, having Jesus in the center of it. On the contrary, when it comes to our relationship with the dead, the Bible clearly states that under no circumstance are we permitted to even allow that thought to cross our mind!

You will not need an extra hour; you have no issues to settle; there is no message allowed to come from the dead towards you or from you to the dead. No, no, no. Never believe this lie. It is a very dangerous lie, a very powerful one, and a very easy one to fall in.

If you ever, by any means, have searched for advice from a dead person or for an extra hour with them, tell your pastor or one of the leaders in the church and have the soul tie that was created broken. Innocent chats about weather, heaven, hell, shopping, house chores, to adoration, worship and sexual encounters with spirits (especially if the deceased was your partner!) all these are included in the serious warnings of the Scripture not to practice them. Any relationship advances towards something, it leads somewhere. If you have ever practiced any of the practices mentioned before, you are in serious danger. There is no need to panic, but decide and act upon it as soon as you realize you were involved in any communication with the dead. I would encourage you to break it in prayer even if you are not sure there is anything to break, because if there is not, you will not have lost anything. But if there is and you will not act against it, you and your family are not safe.

The first step you must take is to lift your eyes to Jesus, look Him in the eye and pray this prayer: "Jesus Christ, Son of God and Lord over my life, I confess that I have lived in a lack of clarity and mind-confusion and have searched for ways to communicate with the dead. I repent of doing it, I turn away from my dependence on anyone other than You, and I ask for Your forgiveness and guidance from this point on. In Your Name I break any spiritual bondage with any spirit that has deceived me and I call on Your Holy Spirit to cleanse me, fill me and guide me. I reckon myself under no other power, authority or influence than Your Holy Spirit. Amen."

If something breaks, you will know. And if it does not, call for help and reinforcement in prayer. It is not a game.

THE "BIG-BOOTS-TO-FILL" LIE

This is one of the lies that that tend to crop up in later widowhood, but it can be planted as a tiny seed in our hearts from the very moment our loved one dies.

People try to say many things when they are in the presence of someone who is suffering. Most of those things are said to avoid awkward silences they feel the need to fill with a really clever line which actually can be completely misguiding. And this is one of the things you will hear often: "*Well... there are some big shoes to fill for whoever comes next in your life...*"

Ideally, people are not buried un-shoed. And although we might have never had the chance to think about burying rituals, they are actually a great proof of what the cultural take on human life is. They reveal the core of what a society thinks about death – hence, the interesting and different rituals of burial in history.

The purpose of this section is not to analyze in detail what we believe as a generation or as a culture about ourselves by the means of burial rituals, but let me point out that in the emotional and spiritual realm you need to be aware that once something has returned to the ground, the ways of living and the reality conditioned by that person's existence is over. If your child died, for no reason why your other child needs to *fill in the shoes* of the one who died. If your spouse has died, there is absolutely no need to bring up the topic of filling her/his boots with your new partner. Comparisons serve no useful purpose. People are unique. Do not even consider getting involved into a new relationship as long as you still have shoes / coats / hats of the past lingering around the house or in your heart. It is not fair towards anyone to have to become someone else (it is not even Biblical!), it is really hurtful for them and it definitely will not help you overcome your fears or have your needs fulfilled. The old is gone, the new has come. - And this new, even if it is a desired or a hated new, was brought in your life and you need to humbly accept it and allow it to make you even more fruitful for the Lord. It may or it may not involve a new child or a new spouse or a new parent. But either it does or it does not, the past was buried with shoes on - and all the emotional attachment symbolized by that pair of shoes - once and for all.

Do not live expecting for someone identical to the loved one who died to come along. Do not live lingering on the past. That is not living; it is a living hell for you and all those around you who are trying to get you out of your depression.

"Lean on, trust in, and be confident in the Lord with all your heart and mind and you will rely on your own insight or understanding. In all your ways know, recognize, and acknowledge Him, and He will direct and make straight and plain your paths" (Proverbs 3:5.)

THE "YOU-ARE-ALONE" LIE

This is one of those lies that are constant lies spoken in our ears by the enemy because it is so easy to fall into, although the Bible says the contrary an overwhelming number of times. Still, from getting the information to living it out, there is a small step, called *mind renewing*. We need to make the conscious effort to believe what the Bible says by the renewing of our mind, although there are times when what the Bible says seems to be so different from what we see happening.

Not only are we told that the Lord is with us, but the Bible makes it clear that He is *in* us and that we are to decide to cast our anxieties onto Him. 1 Peter 5:6,7 says:

"Therefore humble yourselves [demote, lower yourselves in your own estimation] under the mighty hand of God, that in due time He may exalt you, casting the whole of your care [all your anxieties, all your worries, all

your concerns, once and for all] on Him, for He cares for you affectionately and cares about you watchfully."

Matthew 28:18-20:

"Jesus approached and, breaking the silence, said to them, All authority (all power of rule) in heaven and on earth has been given to Me. Go then and make disciples of all the nations, baptizing them into the name of the Father and of the Son and of the Holy Spirit, teaching them to observe everything that I have commanded you, and behold, I am with you all the days (perpetually, uniformly, and on every occasion), to the [very] close and consummation of the age. Amen (so let it be)."

These Scriptures might seem to be very theoretical and distant, because we have heard them so many times before; the truth is that they are actually really hard to believe. When we look around us and we see the reality in the natural realm – especially when it comes to pain and hurt caused by widowhood – it seems as if the Bible impersonal, distant and even insensitive. Especially with women, it can be tremendously difficult to stand on our own two feet after the husband dies because in most cases, the man is still the main provider for the family; when children are involved and there are financial pressures, things get extremely tough. Most of the time people around widows cannot even grasp the intensity and the complexity of the consequences of a husband's death. But if you struggle with this, if you have no one that actually hears and understands what you are saying about the dire circumstance that you were left in, and if you feel as if you are ripped apart and set aside from the rest, there is hope in that situation. Even your feelings of separation and isolation can be motivation for joy.

The Gospels are so simple in transmitting the loving message Jesus left immediately before His ascension. Most of His disciples had already left their families, so they were already set apart from the rest. Jesus spoke powerful words into their lives, words that changed them completely. Just a short time earlier, Jesus spoke about His ascension and most of His disciples abandoned Him. He asks the twelve in John 6:67-70:

"Jesus said to the Twelve, Will you also go away? [And do you too desire to leave Me?] Simon Peter answered, Lord, to whom shall we go? You have

the words (the message) of eternal life. And we have learned to believe and trust, and [more] we have come to know [surely] that You are the Holy One of God, the Christ (the Anointed One), the Son of the living God. Jesus answered them, Did I not choose you, the Twelve?"

But when the moment for His departure finally arrived, His disciples sank into an awkward silence. They had left their homes and their families, they had relinquished everything they had and the way of living that they knew, and now He really appeared to be leaving them as orphans. But right after Jesus's ascension we know that the Holy Spirit filled the disciples and they never again felt alone.

The reality is this: when no one knows what is going on inside you, when no one knows the pain and the hurt you are going through, unless you make the conscious decision to believe Him and trust Him, no one can drag you into that place of faith. Of course, God's grace is undeserved and it is the only means for salvation, manifested through the Cross. But you are the only one who can decide for yourself if you will trust Him to break the "awkward silence". No one can take that decision for you, and no one can influence that decision once it is taken. We cannot convince one another of anything we do not actually want to believe. There is a level up to which we can influence one another, as humans, yes. But that inner decision, the one that is powerful enough to change the course of your thoughts and the actions you take is not under anyone else's power to control. We need to understand that none of the devil's lies are of any effect on us if we decide to believe the Truth, and hang on to believing the Truth in spite of what we see – and that is what faith is.

Believing does not happen randomly. At the foundation of each belief stands a decision (which sometimes is unconscious) to believe whatever we believe. That is why some beliefs are so hard to tear down; not because of the power of the idea itself that we believe in - sometimes what we believe can be an utter lie, which is dead in itself. What empowers whatever we believe is the intensity of the decision we took to believe that particular thing. The grip of the decision to believe that particular thing in which the heart is caught, that is what makes the belief stand strong. And the truth is, if we are honest with ourselves, we know what grips our heart and to what extent. In fact, no one except the owner of the heart truly knows where the heart is.

Let me also submit to you that whatever you decide to believe is what will happen to you not because there is any "magic" in the power of positive thinking, but because this is the power of faith. Any belief that you start acting upon becomes active faith. And even if faith is misused, it is still faith and it still does the same thing God created it to do: it brings into reality what is unseen. This is why it is so important to put our faith in our Lord Jesus Christ, because that faith will draw us nearer to Him.

Hence, if you choose to believe that you are alone, no one and nothing will ever convince that you are *not* alone. If you choose to believe that you are a victim or that you are the pariah, that is what you will live like and that is where you will stay. There are countless examples of people deciding to think about themselves to be more than what they really are, and countless examples of people who have decided to think that they are less than Jesus says. Thinking that you are any different from what He says you are does not mean you are humble, even if you think: "I am okay with being less, I do not need to be all that He says I am." It is still pride. Believing anything other than what He says is actually pride, even if it sounds humble. The reason is that you willingly put aside the value He attributed to you and move from a position of taking the responsibility of investing the gifts He gave you and the person He made you to be in His Kingdom, into a comfort zone where you opt out of doing anything for Him. Having a victim mentality, disbelieving that you are not alone, is not an excuse in His eyes. He already told you that you are not alone. If you choose to believe that you are alone rather than believing Him, it is your choice and you must accept the consequences.

It was in the deepest, darkest moments of my life when I understood that I will have no excuse when I will have to look Him in the eye for not yielding to Him. I will have to answer Him about the way I have stewarded what He invested in me.

The Judgment Day will be painful not because God will bring to light what we did or what we did not do - it is not about deeds! - but because that day He will expose all hearts, without exception. Hence, even the good deeds done with an alternative motive will be exposed. Starting with the Revelation of the Son of God and ending with the revelation of the last baby conceived, all hearts will be exposed in the blink of the eye. No excuse, no wickedness, no double-mildness will be possible starting from that second on because Jesus will shine in His glory. He will break the silence once again.

God will not be deceived and He will not be held accountable by us; we will not bring any accusation against Him and we will not have any chance to put Him on trial: He has already said that we are not alone. Whether we believe it or not, we will reap the consequences of what we actually believe and live in the good of, but no belief of ours will change the reality of what He said. No false reality we create in our mind will stand any longer. At the end of the day, we can try to hide behind a victim mentality, and He will not force us out of it. We can choose to live in the lie of being alone. Or we can choose to live in the reality of His words. We cannot live in both and we cannot decide in which reality anyone else lives. We are responsible for our own hearts.

CHAPTER V

THE JEALOUS GOD, THE DECEITFUL IDOL, THE SELF-ABSORBED WOUNDED AND THE CHILDREN OF WRATH

THE JEALOUS GOD

God's jealousy for His place in our life is limitless. God desires us with jealousy. Our spouse and our family are gifts from Him, but when we invest more heart and we pour ourselves more into anything other than Him, these things become idols.

Let us look at some Scriptures together:

Exodus 34:14: "You will not worship any other god, for the Lord, Whose name is Jealous, is a jealous God."

Exodus 20:5: "You shall not bow down to them or worship them; for I, the Lord your God, am a jealous God, punishing the children for the sin of the parents to the third and fourth generation of those who hate Me, but showing love to a thousand generations of those who love Me and keep My commandments."

The Bible goes on and on about God's jealousy - Joshua 24:19; 1 Kings 14:22; Psalm 78:58; Psalm 79:5; Proverbs 27:4, Deuteronomy 4:20, Deuteronomy 5:8-10, Deuteronomy 6:14-15, Deuteronomy 32:12.

God's ultimate manifestation of jealousy was through Jesus. We tend to see the Son of God as a shy village boy growing up among carpenters and contemplating nature. It is true that Jesus was excited about everything God the Father created, but His contemplation of nature and earth and humanity was not limited to feelings of beatitude, but provoked wrath: until the time of Jesus, God kept saying through the prophets that He is jealous. Jesus came and became God's jealousy manifested on earth, living and breathing among us. Jesus was controversial to the point of turning upside down the entire business developed around the sacrificial system, because the sacrificial system that God himself gave the pattern for was being strictly obeyed but for the wrong reasons. God's intention with the Law was that the Israelites would hear His heart-beat. Throughout the entire Law section of the Bible, you can almost hear God saying: "My heart beats for justice; My heart beats for love; My heart beats for holiness; My heart beats for a relationship with you; My heart beats for love." The Law is all about finding satisfaction in God and being satisfied in Him, not about being satisfied in fulfilling a ritual or reciting a series of prayers.

If we look in Proverbs chapter 6 v. 34-35 and chapter 7, v.13-20 we see what the fulfilling of God's Law became: a self-satisfying act that allowed more sin to be committed.

"She took hold of him and kissed him and with a brazen face she said: "Today I fulfilled my vows, and I have food from my fellowship offering at home. So I came out to meet you; I looked for you and have found you! I have covered my bed with colored linens from Egypt. I have perfumed my bed with myrrh, aloes and cinnamon. Come, let us drink deeply of love till morning; Let us enjoy ourselves with love! My husband is not at home; he has gone on a long journey. He took his purse filled with money and will not be home till full moon.""

"For jealousy arouses a husband's fury, and he will show no mercy when he takes revenge. He will not accept any compensation; he will refuse a bribe, however great it is."

In our "good prayers", when we ask for the things that we think are good (including the life of our loved ones) and we justify our prayers that are meant to satisfy our desires and not God's purpose, using the "because you are good" formula, we actually do the same thing: we have an ill founded relationship with God, like that of the adulterous woman had with her husband. We go to God and we pray because we need to pray to make ourselves feel better and get what we want from Him: liberation and intervention according to our own wishes and desires. That is not what prayers are for. Our prayers are to be the intimate acts of communication with God, during which we willingly recognize that His ways are better than ours and we align our hearts with His will. The primary purpose of prayer is not to make God happy and then go our own way, like the purpose of the sacrificial system was not to make God happy and then go and commit adultery. We are the ones who need redemption and adjustment to His will, for He does not need to hear and see how we praise Him. God does not need any of that; He is secure in who He is. We are the ones who depend on Him. God is not dependent on our prayers.

There's a very interesting verse in Hebrews 5:7; it says:

"In the days of His flesh [Jesus] offered up definite, special petitions [for that which He not only wanted [but needed] and supplications with strong crying and tears to Him Who was [always] able to save Him [out] from death, and He was heard because of His reverence toward God [His godly fear, His piety, [in that He shrank from the horrors of separation from the bright presence of the Father]."

In other words, Jesus's prayers were answered while He was on Earth because He not only asked for the things He needed (not the ones He wanted!), but because He shrank back from the horrors of separation from the bright presence of the Father. Jesus was heard because He wanted to stay in an intimate relationship with the Father. Regardless of what the other options were (dominion, kingship, and everything the adversary tempted Him with in the wilderness), He understood that these other options implied the bitterness of being separated from the Father. However glamorous the riches of this world (including the glamour of a marital status!), they are not worth separation from God's presence. God was Jesus's focus. God really was Jesus's heart desire. In 1 Thessalonians 5:22 we are taught to do the same:

"Abstain from evil [shrink from it and keep aloof from it] in whatever form or whatever kind it may be."

Our reason to pursue God should never be the things He gives us (including people), nor even what we need. Expect God to neglect your fears and anxieties and complaints and constantly ask you during the hardest trials: "What about US?" (in which case, by US he means you and Him). And sometimes, yes, it will even seem as if He does not care at all about you and cannot be bothered with your smallness when actually He wants you to focus your eyes on Him because when you are looking straight at Him, you are opening your life to His healing.

It is true that we do get feelings of being strengthened in prayer because God rejoices when we develop our relationship with God in the way that He was intended, but that is not why we should open up to Him. In the book of Nehemiah, chapter 8 verse 8-10, we see that when the Word of God impacts people and they repent and allow their hearts to be aligned to the Will of the Father, this fine-tuning with God's will brings them strength:

*"They (*the Levites) read from the Book of the Law of God, making it clear and giving the meaning so that the people understood what was being read. Then Nehemiah the governor, Ezra the priest and teacher of the Law, and the Levites who were instructing the people said to them all, "This day is holy to the Lord your God. You will mourn or weep." For all the people had been weeping as they listened to the words of the Law. Nehemiah said, "Go and enjoy choice food and sweet drinks, and send some to those who have nothing prepared. This day is holy to our Lord. You will grieve, for the joy of the Lord is your strength.""*

The joy of enjoying choice of food and sweet drinks comes after repentance, which is brought by having all idols cast out and having the hearts pierced by the spirit of the Law, not by the rituals of the Law. The fact that the Levites explained what the Law was shows that true repentance comes in spirit, not in mindless observance of rituals. It comes as a consequence of real, complete devotion and self-implication in understanding God.

Any desire (other than the desire to pursue God) taken to extreme, good or bad, is rebellion against God's will. The thing that we see as good might be good in the short term, but not in the long term. And even if it is good in the long term, in human perception,

God might want a different good for us – He never wants bad things for us. If you ever experience doubts in dialogues between you and God, doubt only yourself and the rightness of your desires, not Him.

Let us take a look at what the Bible considers to be rebellion, hence sin: there are two ways of being in rebellion against God. The New Testament reveals this in the parable of the lost son (Luke 15:11-32).

There is a type of rebellion that is obvious - and the culture seems to believe the answer to it is education – because it affects a rather large number of people and is committed not only against God but also against humans and it harms them at the level of personal needs (physiological security and safety needs). This kind of rebellion attacks the *nature* of God, desiring the things that God dislikes, to take an extreme example, a serial killer: the entire social immune system, represented by any way of catching such a person (police, media, internet, etc.), would be alerted and would react. Nobody wants such a psychopath to claim another victim. This modern culture might not like God, but it still holds high the traits of His nature, like safety, security, protection, love.

There's a second type of rebellion, which attacks the *ways* of God. Wanting good things for the wrong reasons and obtaining them by ways that are not godly, is in God's eyes as wrong as wanting the wrong things. This sin affects humans on the other levels of fundamental needs (belonging, esteem and self-actualization). Yet since the effects impact only those close to the sinner, society often excuse the person saying "The end justifies the means.". Take for example abortion. We do not see it as a sin in modern society because we are not affected, as neighbors, by the mother that has multiple abortions nor of the children that no one hears screaming and whose bodies are not found under a bush. We might see it as inappropriate and we might try to advise our daughters not to do so, but we would not alert the police or the mass-media and the case would not go viral on internet like that of the serial killer. This sin is silent and even when noticed it does not arouse any sense of urgency in society – or it rarely does so. Of course, God's will is not to have orphans and children growing up without a father. So a woman's desire not to raise a child alone is a good one. But God's way of solving the issue is not by killing the unborn, but by stopping their mothers sleeping with guys without being married to them. Humans not wanting fatherless children are right, but the way we choose to prevent that from happening is not to stop the sin of adultery but to kill the fruit of sin. We stop sin by sinning. In this case, we want the same thing as God does, but we do it differently. And when it comes to holiness or ungodliness, there is no room for creativity to sort out our sins: living outside God's ways and purposes is a sin. Living a lifestyle that is outside the lifestyle of God is a sin; we were created to have His lifestyle. That is what we were created for: to reflect His image and likeness. Failing to live in His image and likeness, be it intentional or unintentional, is called by the Bible to be living in sin. God defines Himself and He defined what human nature should be like when He created us in His image and likeness. In other words, even if our intentions are good, God places a great value on the method that we use in order to fulfill them, not only on the desire in itself.

Let us look in the Bible at the example of rebellion mentioned before.

The so called prodigal son does not want what his father wants; he does not want to work, nor does he desire structure and morality in his life. He fancies spending money with women, throwing parties and living a depraved life. Because he cannot have this lifestyle in his father's house, he decides to leave. The other son, on the contrary, desires the title of "the good son", loves being appreciated for what he does and delights in the title that he has in his father's house, but he does not want these for the reasons nor by the ways his father implemented in the household. He wants these things for the benefits that they bring to him, personally. When these good things cease to make him the center of attention (oh, the fattened calf that was killed for that rebellious brother of his instead of him!), he gets angry because of the goodness of his father's heart. His rebellion manifests itself as selfishness.

Jesus obviously tries to warn us that desiring things that God dislikes is no less a sin than desiring the good things that God desires but for the bad reasons and obtaining them in ungodly ways. Both sons wanted to gain what they liked, they just liked different things: one liked a depraved lifestyle, the other one wanted glory obtained by robotically fulfilling his father's desires, rather than having his heart in tune with his father's.

I would encourage you to look at the root of your desire when you plead for someone's life. Yes, I pleaded for my father's life for over a decade, and yes, I pleaded for my husband's life with panic for the two minutes that I had available. Yes, it is natural, it is normal; it is not sinful as a first reaction. But when God decides not to honor that plea because our ways are not His, if our hearts turns bitter towards God instead of trusting in Him, we are in sin. There might be holy people that honestly want their loved ones to live because they were useful in the Kingdom of God on Earth and there is so much left to do for God, but generally that is not the reason why we want our loved ones to live. We would have wanted them to live because we needed their company for ourselves.

In a strange way, that becomes clear when someone that is not really close to us but is really helpful to us dies or relocates. When a decent Christian mechanic who charges fair prices for his work dies, he will be missed by his customers not because he could have become much holier for the glory of God, but because he provided a quality service that they needed.

When Claudiu died, one of his contacts told me: "In a selfish way, I was thinking yesterday evening that now that Claudiu's gone, I will not have anyone to send me links on various topics that I'll preach on.". Do you see the irony here? Everything that lives and exists does so for the glory of God. As Christians, we promote that idea. But do we really believe it when He decides to do whatever He pleases with what belongs to Him? Do we really believe it when His being Lord means we need to accept hurting and suffering as a consequence of His will?

Of course we hate death, and of course we shouldn't go through widowhood as if nothing happened. A lot happens inside us and outside us when someone dies. And it is a big deal. Of course we ask our Father to grant us the company of our loved ones. I am not trying to militate for a Christianity that lacks emotions. But I am militating for a heart that is honest and completely raw and broken in relationship with God. We cannot fool God, pretending that we worship Him and actually having idols. We might not be aware of our idols, but if we are open for Him to show us our idols, He will. We can, however, at any time, choose not to see them and to fight against the One who exposes them.

Why is God *so* jealous about the place He has in your life? Because the place you assign to Him says what you actually believe about Him. When you believe the wrong things about Him, you put Him in the wrong place. If you know and believe the truth about Him, you will put Him in the right place in your life, and the fact that you place Him there enables Him to act in the fullness of who He is in your life. You need to know that whatever is good comes from Him. He will not share His glory with anyone else, so He will refrain from being who He is and He will limit His working in your life if the praise will be wrongly accredited. And if you think about it, that is grace because in that way He prevents you from having your idol confirmed. In other words, He wants to have the right place in your life because that releases the fullness of who He is in you. He is not a narcissistic being that needs to have His identity confirmed or He will be cross with you and face a severe identity crisis. He wants you to know who He is because it benefits you and your children.

Do you truly believe with all your heart, in spite of everything you see or feel that God is completely good and pure and cannot be tempted to do evil? Do you really trust Him to jump in the stormy waters if He brings you to the edge of the shore? Are you completely confident in God's character? Do you believe God is pure? If you do not actually believe all these, may I suggest that for your own good, you take your unbelief to Him. God's promises are never based on our efforts or on whom we are, but on who He is, because He is the one who promises and loves first, not us. And if you want to be healed, position yourself appropriately. Cold-bloodedly grab your aching heart and bring it into obedience to Christ. Change position. Hurt and barely breathing as you may be, move towards Him. Do not wait to fix yourself and then go to Him, because you will never do it; you will just sink in your imperfection, instead of being launched into His healing holiness.

THE DECEITFUL IDOL

In the previous chapter we looked at some of the lies the devil tells us. In this section we will examine two others, as I find them to be very apparent in the Body of Christ and widely accepted, although they are so dangerous and often wrapped in a cloak of piety and humility.

One of the greatest dangers that threaten the Church - and history confirms that this practice has been common to a degree throughout the ages - is the worship of the dead.

Christians are taught that we are worshipers – and that is true. It is often debated what worship is; and that is a good thing, because there will always be someone who will think that going to church makes him a worshiper, forgetting that going under water does not make anyone a fish. But in addition to that, we need to understand what it is that which makes us worshipers, that special capacity we have that no other beings have, that enables us to worship and (consequently) makes a worship-lifestyle impossible to avoid. If God is not the one we worship, we will surely end up worshiping someone or something else, because we simply cannot choose not to worship just as we cannot choose not to eat.

HOW DO YOU TELL IF YOU WORSHIP A DEAD PERSON?

The Bible defines worship by its symptoms, so that we will be able to recognize it when it happens; here are some of them: reflecting someone (by living a lifestyle similar to theirs), seeking acceptance and company, seeking guidance, living in the shadow of someone, dedicating excessive time to someone.

In other words, if you live a life that imitates the lifestyle of someone whom you loved and died, you are trying to reflect that someone's image, not God's. That is idolatry.

If you express your emotions in a way that would be pleasing to someone who has died, you actually perform rituals of remembrance; it is idolatry because you are seeking acceptance from someone other than Christ.

If you seek the guidance of someone who is dead by speaking to them or by having dreams about them – or if you ask for directive dreams and act upon the "sign" that you get from that certain someone, you are placing at least a measure of unconditional trust in someone other than Christ. (And for sure, you will find yourself listening to a demon, not to the person you think you are listening.)

If you are living in the unseen reality that someone's existence creates, you place your faith in someone other than Christ. Again, that is a form of idolatry.

If you frenetically keep going to the cemetery and keep playing the video from the funeral, or if by missing a daily visit to the cemetery you feel guilty, you are worshiping a dead person.

Your imagination was not given to you so that you would sink into your sofa on a Sunday afternoon, creating scenarios in your head about what you could have done on that specific day with the one who died. We have memories that God in His grace decides sometimes to allow us to keep or in other cases causes our memory to block them, but whatever the case they only bring true comfort if they are brought back to our mind by the Holy Spirit.

Do not speak to the dead; someone will eventually answer, and it will definitely not be the one you think it is, and it definitely will not be God. God has a Name, and unless you call out His name, it is not Him answering. Spirituality is not necessarily Christian; there are many kind of spiritual experiences which are outside what God allows. If we think that non-Christians lack spiritual experiences we live in a bubble of ignorance and we seriously need to gain perspective as a Church. Spirituality has never been as trendy as it is today.

Do not engage in intimacy – alone or with another partner – thinking about the dead one. That is a deadly snare. It probably is the most slippery slope of all. Do not allow sensual thoughts about the dead person in your mind. Take captive every thought and make it obedient to God.

Relics, shrines and rituals of remembrance are disgusting to God. They are the ultimate reflection of idolatry, yet they have filled churches for centuries. The worship of dead people has gained a lot of emphasis in the last centuries because its development was facilitated by the cultural paradigm shift from a rational society to a spiritual-experience based culture.

Do not make decisions based on "What would that person think? What would s/he like?" – Do not ever buy anything for the reason that that person liked it or you think it would have liked it. That is pleasing the dead; it is another form of idolatry.

Dead people do not speak. Dead people do not give advice and do not have preferences as to the music you listen, to the food that you eat, the clothes you wear. Dead pets do not make sounds. They may appear to be present and may make you feel guilty for not answering when they call or for not recognizing them, but this is the activity of lying demons. Do not engage in conversations with them. Call on Jesus and they will flee away. No matter how deep and severe your pain is, do not engage in any spiritual activity with anyone else than Bible-believing Christians and Christ.

Do not pray for dreams about that person. The enemy gives dreams as well, and if you cry out for dreams because you want to emotionally rest in those dreams instead of resting in God, you are opening the door to nightmares. And it is idolatry!

From what I have seen in so many cases, the rooms of the dead ones have become shrines soon after their death. Cleaning the house as soon as possible and giving away quickly the belongings of Claudiu has helped me a lot. I didn't even realize how much healing that will bring in my life. It might help you as well not to keep the room of the deceased intact – it will prevent it from becoming a shrine. Change as much as you possibly can, if that is what helps you shift your focus from the loved one who has passed away on to God. Selling a house or a car to make way for the Holy Spirit to take control over your life rather than the memory of the deceased one is not "too extreme". It might be exactly what you need at that point, in which case it is being faithful and running with all your strength to God; He will honor it. Do not allow your heart to slip away on the path of self-pity and self-absorption.

Make sure you check your heart even if you cannot specifically recall doing any of these things. Ask the Holy Spirit to bring to light whether you ever allowed any form of idolatry into your life.

Remember, worship is not about the worshiper, it is about the one who is worshiped. When someone who used to trigger good feelings in us – someone who loved us and whom we loved – is taken away, if we act on the premise that we should be self-oriented and egocentric, we will seek for that person's presence even if s/he is dead. We may even have such feelings towards a family pet. That is how weak we are in discernment because of all the voices that we listen to. Anything that makes you focus on your pain, anything that keeps coming back to you to oppress you, anything that makes you turn in bitterness from God, needs to go. If someone's death enrages you to the point where you reject God, that is a very clear sign of having a idol.

When someone dies, the physical and the spiritual reality change – and so does the emotional reality. Walk away with God from the old reality because the soul of the loved one is no longer among the living ones in body, and if you keep doing the things that you did with the loved one (walks, chats, laughter, sharing, sending them e-mails, sending them letters, etc.) in the spiritual realm which now is void of that person's presence, someone will fill the void left by their departure, and it is not a benevolent spirit.

The danger of worshiping the dead was always present in the institutional Church in various forms, because we were not called to worship any other human (dead or alive) than Jesus. Worshiping icons, statues or relics - all of these are acts of idolatry. But in the last centuries, as we have shown before, the danger increased by the fact that the culture taught us that it is not about a collectivity but about "ME": my experience, my pain, my prayer, my conversation with my own Savior – who can be my dad, my husband, my child – dead or alive. The Church needs to learn to bury their dead. We believe in resurrection. We need to understand that we have to trust God with the lives of the ones that we love and with our emotions as well. Nothing is lost in Christ, no one perishes. They will all be resurrected, but we need to bury them!

If the devil can convince us that we can somehow meet with the ones who have died, he has won the battle. Instead running to Christ, who is Alive and defines this world by His existence, we slip onto the ground that is defined by the existence of the deceased one. Have you ever heard people saying: "I am doing this because my daughter who died two years ago would have liked me to do this?" – That is a pretty good indicator of worship: the desire to please a dead person. If the one that the worship is directed to is not alive, the devil will wear the mask of that person and take advantages, gradually seizing ground and authority. Remember, God does not wear masks of any kind. Never.

When Claudiu died, I looked up for forums for widows, looking for advice and fellowship. And I found loads of bad advice on how to keep alive the memory of the dead: there were two women (mother and daughter) that decided to give away gifts on the street on their husband's and dad's birthday. They did that for over 20 years. And my question was – "why would we seek to keep alive the memory of the dead?" You see, if you allow God to heal you, it does not mean that you wake up one morning not remembering anything about your past. It means, though, that the memory of the loved one will fall like a piece of a puzzle into the right place that God desires and it will not come at you as a power that oppresses you and demands obedience from you. You do not need to struggle with organizing your life, your heart or your emotions around a memory – Jesus puts the memory where it should be in a healthy way that is *safe* for you, a way that will not turn the deceased into an idol.

In Deuteronomy chapter 18, verse 9-14, God warns His people

about the spiritual customs of the land they were to take over, and tells them not to join in with the natives of the land:

""When you come into the land which the Lord your God is giving you, you shall not learn to follow the abominations of those nations. There shall not be found among you anyone who makes his son or his daughter pass through the fire, or one who practices witchcraft, or a soothsayer, or one who interprets omens, or a sorcerer, or one who conjures spells, or a medium, or a spiritist, or one who calls up the dead. For all who do these things are an abomination to the Lord, and because of these abominations the Lord your God drives them out from before you. You shall be blameless before the Lord your God. For these nations which you will dispossess listened to soothsayers and diviners; but as for you, the Lord your God has not appointed such for you."

Yes, embracing pain is definitely part of the healing process, but when embracing pain becomes a lifestyle, a way of living, a way of dragging yourself through life, it is a sin and it is a form of idolatry. Our way of living is not based on embracing pain, but on embracing holiness. And this is one of the greatest secrets that the Bible teaches us: when you embrace something long enough, that something embraces you back. When you embrace holiness, holiness embraces you back; when you embrace pain, pain embraces you back; when you embrace sin, sin embraces you back. In James 4:8a we read:

"Draw near to God and He will draw near to you".

The law of attraction is equally valid for sin: draw near to pain and pain will draw near to you. This is exactly why we should draw near to God because no matter what draws near to us, if we draw near to Him, His presence will drive out all other influences. He will draw near to us and the mere fact that He is there will surely consume all pain, all darkness and all confusion. He is the Light of the world. If you want to choose to live your life in the hell of pain, do not blame God. Repent of embracing pain for too long, draw near to God, and His presence will make the pain go away without any doubt – just as light makes darkness go away not by force but merely by what light is.

Part of God's Fatherhood is the fact that He corrects us and He brings us back. Being aware that you put God in the wrong place or being aware there was a man in God's place in your life does not mean you are doomed – it means God loves you and used the pain in your life lovingly to point out the wrong in the ways of your heart so He would have your acceptance to change the ways of your heart. He wants you under His authority because it is under His authority that He has the possibility to be your defender and your redeemer. He does not rebuke you, He tells you to let go of whatever you were holding on to so that He could fill that space and be your defender. Do not feel condemned, rejected or unwanted – feel loved, deeply loved.

THE SELF-ABSORBED WOUNDED

While Naomi – self-called Mara – declares with her own mouth that her identity has changed for the worse, according to her marital status, her parenting status and her wealth (and she blames God for all these!), Ruth does not declare anything but she acts as a woman that is still completely sure about her identity in Christ whom she met through conversion. Naomi is bitter and self-absorbed; Ruth is standing firm as a rock: she is there to help even though she is in the same circumstances as Naomi, and even worse because she was a young Moabite widow, childless, that has previously been married to an Israelite so neither Moabites nor Israelites would have been happy with that confused situation. But God was pleased with her heart and she knew that true acceptance comes from God, not from her nation nor the Israelites nor from bearing children, nor even from being married or not. This is what makes Ruth so special that she was accepted in the genealogy of Jesus and she has an entire book of the Bible named after her: she believed she was accepted in Christ and she faithfully walked in that acceptance in spite of all circumstances. And when widowhood came, she was not shaken. Helping your bitter mother-in-law is not your first reaction unless you know for sure your identity was not in a person. In other words, her identity changed when she met Christ, not when her husband died. If our identity is changed when we meet Christ, that is the only change that we experience and that defines our entire life from that point on. There is only one change of identity that stands against any circumstance, and that is the change of whatever identity we have, into the identity we have in Christ. And it is only when we know who we are in Christ that we are able to help even when we are afflicted. It is Christ that helps through us. And if Christ works through us, we are not required to be in top shape; we can be afflicted and wounded, but available – and He will honor that availability by using us and making it easy for us to bear fruit; that is what Christ does through Ruth with Naomi.

THE CHILDREN OF WRATH

The best thing a single parent can do for her/his children is not related to material status or fulfilling their needs which the other parent should have fulfilled. Do not try to replace the one who died and do not try to buy your children out of mourning by spoiling them with gifts which are beyond their age whether in terms of finance or responsibility (cars, motorcycles, apartments, accepting boyfriends / girlfriends to move in, etc.). Anger is not caused only by the absence of a parent, it is also caused by the inability to change things, and this inability will only be underlined by such a behavior on your part.

When it comes to roles in the family, lack of role definition only leads to excruciating confusion in your children's minds. Traumas such as divorce and death are very much amplified by the role confusion that the adults in their lives go through. Trying to be who we aren't or trying to excuse God for what He does in the family will not bare good fruit; but rather, if we teach the children to walk in obedience and trust Him, we can be sure that God will fill the gap created by death. He will surely pour Himself out to them. If you try to fill the gap with yourself, your children will either end up confused about what a family is supposed to be like or go through the painful experience of emotional incest in addition to the original pain.

We live in a time when there's a massive spiritual attack on the issue of gender and identity. Until a child has enough maturity to be able to make the distinction between an individual, the role that individual has and his acts, it might take a really long time. A child will not have the reflex to analyze the dynamic of the family, and to decide if it is dysfunctional or not. He is not equipped with the right tools to do so.

The Israelites were taught to teach their children who they were, where they came from, their relationship with God, and the Law. And this was not for God's benefit, this was for the benefit of the following generations; they needed to know who they were. They needed to learn to stand firm in the identity that God established in them, so they would not give up protecting the land that God established them in.

If you want to protect your children from the gender attack that will surely come, especially in the case of young children that lose one of their parents, you need to be who you are, leave a vacuum in the place of the one that is not there, and allow God to use that space as He wishes. He might eventually send someone to fill that space or He will fill it Himself. Just trust Him. Trusting God is not as easy as it sounds.

Do not take your children into a place of confusion because when they will be mature enough to understand what happened when they lost a parent, they will turn against you if you repeatedly sinned against them trying to be who you are not. Do not lead them into believing that they are stuck with a parent who is uncertain of who s/he is and with a God that pretty much has no opinion on the issues - or if He does love them, He is too weak to intervene and He has to push forth a wounded widow to save the day because He cannot do it Himself. Do not sabotage their relationship with Jesus. You are not a super-parent and Jesus is not a tiny boy in a manger. Let Him be the super-hero of the story of their life, and their hearts will turn back with trust to God. If you attempt to be the super-hero, they will turn back with bitterness towards God and later on, with anger towards you. If you are a woman and you need to move, with 3 small children and no father, call for help and teach the children: "Dad is not here, but God is a good Father to us and He provided men to help us move the heavy furniture. God hears us when we call." Make a point of showing them specifically and practically how God fills in the gaps. If you are a man and you have lost your wife, be sure God will send someone to help with cleaning and cooking. If there's no human there to listen, He will send ravens. He will not desert you. And when He does deliver, make sure you teach your child that God has heard you. That builds their confidence in God. We expect our children to trust God but we forget that we need to teach them how to do that. My dad was my greatest teacher: I saw all his pain and suffering, and I have not heard him even once to say that God had abandoned him, although surely that was what my childish eyes saw. No, he kept teaching me that God is there and we see Him by faith. My father's faith is one of the stones that God placed in the foundation of my being, and it is unshakeable because my father was unshaken in his faith. That is there to stay for eternity. That is solid ground which I was taught how to step on. That was parenting coming from a man's personal relationship with Jesus that impacted his daughter in her childhood.

It is essential to understand that your parenting will come from your relationship with Jesus. And that is how things should be even prior to your spouse's death: parenting comes from how you walk with Jesus. Any parenting comes from relationship with Jesus, but when your parenting is placed under the magnifying glass of widowhood and pain, that is even clearer.

Do not bring lies about God into your children's lives by trying to sort out their feelings. Do not tell them by your actions that Jesus is not their Savior, that God the Father is not a Father. The devil works day and night for that – you need to teach them the truth. You need to work with God. Even if the orphans whose Father He becomes directly are your children, they still fall under all the privileges written in the Bible, and if you lie to them – intentionally or not, by commission or omission – all the effects of God's protection will be there for them, but against you. Sometimes we relate strangely to a family member when they go through pain, because we fail to understand that although we are like a family in Christ, eventually every single one of us is in Christ and responsible for her/himself, and Christ is impacting one individual at a time. If your children are orphans and you harm them, even if you are a widow, God will protect them from you if He has to. And if your orphan children harm you as a widow, He will protect you from them. And that is a good thing because where there are many wounds, there are many reactions which have the potential to harm.

God will not let anyone take His place, and He clearly and repeatedly says that He is the Father of the fatherless. Do not be self-absorbed to the point that you start taking over Jesus's place in their life. The best thing you can do for them when their other parent is gone is the best thing you can do when they still have their other parent as well as you: be secure about who you are in Christ, be confident about it, and God will be everything that you are not. He will bring completion to your work if you allow Him to do so. Walk your walk with Jesus and that will be the safe ground for them to develop their own walk with Jesus. If you are constantly in panic mode and find yourself paralyzed, bewildered, insecure or unwilling to heal, your children will never know Who they are building on and the devil will use that uncertainty and confusion that you spread to attack them.

CHAPTER VI

WHAT WIDOWHOOD
IS AND IT IS NOT

The week that followed my husband's death was surreal. After I finally got two hours' sleep, I woke up at my aunt's house, scared and alone. I looked at the ceiling; I looked around; nothing seemed familiar: "Where am I? What happened?" I was not able to gather my thoughts and to at least make sense of the room I was in. It was a feeling that I have experienced a lot in the following weeks.

Extreme pain and panic can trigger extreme reactions. These reactions are either sinful or sanctifying. Revenge, depression, substance abuse, sexual sin, gluttony, etc., are justified by world's understanding of pain even if they are taken to a radical level. But the true radical action is to refuse to let go of God, despite the agony that you are going through. If we live by the laws of the flesh, there is no way we will make the right decisions – especially when we are vulnerable!

Although it is in our nature to sin, the Bible does not approve a less holy life style when we are hurt. If we do not know who the Lord is, what He has done for us and what He expects from us, we slide.

Two months after my husband died, I realized that I was a stranger to myself. I have never previously experienced self-awareness to that degree. As an artist, I do have a powerful personal introspection mechanism and I knew the Ligia I was before my husband died. But now it seemed that not only the surrounding reality had changed, but even I had suddenly changed. And every time I would try to spend time with myself and heal my wounds or meditate on God's Word, I would realize that I no longer was who I believed I was. I discovered aspects of myself that I was not even aware were there. I did not even know how to be myself, I was not sure what happened to the former me that I was friends with and it felt as if my entire identity had changed. No one told me that when you bury your husband the extreme emotional distress might alter your behavior, it may alter the way that you relate to others and it alters life itself. But the more I thought about it, the more it made sense. We are already familiar with the social and psychological studies that reveal how events happening throughout life affect us from infancy till the day we die. There might be seasons in life when we can be more perceptive, sensitive and open to change but even after our personalities are fully developed we are still subject to change if we suffer emotional traumas. We are changeable and extreme circumstances will lead to extreme reactions.

The good news is that it is nothing wrong with being changeable. This is the wonderful way we were created to be like; it allows the Holy Spirit to work in us. The Holy Spirit uses this attribute of changeability that we possess to glorify the Lord. The more we are open to the work of the Holy Spirit, the more we are transformed to be like Jesus. The Holy Spirit knows who Jesus is and until the revelation of Jesus Christ is complete in us, He teaches us who He is. This process of learning is vital to every Christian because the enemy also knows that we are changeable especially when we are vulnerable, hence he tries to use our malleability against us. He does not only hate Jesus, and His workmanship in us and His works; he hates us personally. As long as we are in Christ, we are a threat to him.

The initial sin in the Garden of Eden was a consequence of the fact the Adam and Eve did not know who God is, they did not know the character of God – hence, they believed that they would become like God when in fact, they were already made in His likeness (see Genesis 1:26 vs. Genesis 3:5). If they knew what God is like, they would have trusted Him because He is trustworthy. Remember, He does not change, but we do.

God knows that without knowing Him we cannot trust Him more than we would trust a stranger so He repeatedly calls us to get to know Him and He gladly wants to reveal Himself to us (Psalm 34:8 – "Taste and see that the Lord is good; blessed is the one who takes refuge in Him."; John 5; Mathew 11:28). We need to put our roots deep "into Him", we need to have the same Spirit that He does, we need to have fellowship with Him, to be constantly connected to Him in order to be like Him. That is our identity: He is "I AM" and we are "made in His image".

As a result, the mindset that we are encouraged to develop as Christians whilst we mature in Christ is one of complete trust in the Lord. Our security in Him is not allowed to be conditioned by the circumstances that we live in or by our fears (Psalm 91). The question is not if we are changed by pain or not, the question is *whom do our changes reflect?* Do they reflect Christ in us?

Post-modernism has wrongly taught us that emotions are the main criteria by which we should embrace a particular faith or a lifestyle. 2 Timothy 4:3 warns us that

"[…] the time will come when people will not put up with sound doctrine. Instead, to suit their own desires, they will gather around them a great number of teachers to say what their itching ears want to hear."

The culture that we live in surely validates and accepts as a true fact whatever pleases the ones who created the culture.

Paul's writing to the Romans in chapter 12 verse 2 echoes the same idea: if we conform to the cultural pattern we will not be able to test and approve – hence, to discern – God's will.

"You will conform to the pattern of this world, but be transformed by the renewing of your mind. Then you will be able to test and approve what God's will is—his good, pleasing and perfect will."

Christ assures us repeatedly that we will go through troubles – we cannot avoid pain and suffering, but we can react to pain and suffering either in a way that is pleasing to the Lord or in a way that is culturally acceptable as being right. These are the two lenses through which we can see the world: the Bible's perspective or the cultural perspective. In crisis moments it is crucial to know what to do. Imagine a warship caught in the middle of a storm – there's no place for second guesses. A wrong decision can be fatal. Know your direction in life and build on what Christ has already revealed to you about Himself.

The reality is that in dire circumstances our hearts are open and we can clearly see what is inside. And out of all the pain I went through (my father died when I was 15, my husband died when I was 25, I went through a really tough culture shock at 29), my widowhood was the greatest opportunity to look God in the eye and be changed. You can also look God in the eye and change according to who He is, or look Him in the eye and turn away from Him in bitterness.

There are only two heart reactions possible to the challenge of widowhood and death: either change according to His image and likeness, or change according to the patterns of the world.

WHAT WIDOWHOOD IS

Going through widowhood is like going through a magnifying glass. It will show you where you are in your relationship with God, it will show you the deepest recesses of your heart, it will show you who or what you trust in, and it will definitely put you in a situation where you have to make choices.

YOUR WIDOWHOOD IS THE MAGNIFYING GLASS THAT WILL SHOW YOU WHO YOU REALLY ARE AND WHO YOU REALLY BELIEVE GOD IS.

We are in a constant process of learning and developing, and especially as Christians we should be very much aware that our walk with God does not end the moment we decide to follow Him. That is where it all starts. From that point on, we reckon ourselves dead, and we live knowing that the One who leads is the Lord. Deciding to follow Christ means that we accept His invitation to go with

Him in the great adventure of life, on the path that He chooses for us. During this adventure, Christ does not want us to become wobbly or apathetic. The image that we have about Christ carrying us on His back is true for some of the moments of our lives, but we cannot constantly refuse to take responsibility for our lives and our development in Him. He wants to create in us a mature and healthy spiritual being, who is aware of the spiritual realities, and who is also a fighter who takes responsibility. The way we have relationships between us is similar to the way that we are to relate to Him: there is a progression in the intimacy that we have with Christ. There is a deepening in our relationship with Him, which we should pursue.

Of course during our walk with Him trials come, but if we are friends with Him and we trust Him, our reaction will not be to run away from Him, but to run towards Him! That is the normality of the Christian life and that is what David speaks about when he says that he made the Lord his tower of refuge! But if we are not intentional in our relationship with Christ, if we do not "tune in" daily to the Scriptures and if we do not seek to know God's heart merely out of love for Him, if we do not desire to know the very thoughts of Christ, if we are not falling in love with the Person that He is, we will fall apart when something dramatic happens.

How honest are you in your relationship with Christ? How well do you know Him? When the enemy comes and whispers in your ear: "He does not care. He will fail you. He does not listen – He never listens!" – do you believe what the enemy tells you, or do you believe the blood of Christ that speaks louder than any lie?

We cannot *always* ask "Who is God *for you*?"; this question can be of value in certain periods of life, but the question that we should really ask ourselves is "Who is God?"

Do you believe God is love? – Allow me to suggest that "God is love" does *not* mean "Love is God". Do you believe He is the Person who hears you, or do you think His presence is necessarily accompanied by fuzzy warm feelings? Is He the Person who heals you or is He your healing? Do you believe He is not the One who is harming you, or do you secretly say in your heart: *"Well, there's nothing much I can do, God was mean and unjust with me and took my husband away, so now I have to bow my head, not make any nasty remarks towards God and just shut Him out of my life."*

Do you secretly believe that He sinned against you when He allowed your loved one to die? Do you secretly believe He is too busy to spend time with you? Do you think He is absent or overwhelmed by circumstances? Do you think He is a Father who abandons His children?

There is a clear distinction between the two questions "Who is Jesus *for you?*" and "Who is Jesus?" and it is crucial to understand the difference. The first question deals with our personal perception of Him and the answers are based mostly on our personal experiences with Him. The answers to that question lead to amazing testimonies and proofs about how God got involved in someone's life in a particular circumstance. But His particular will for someone's life is not to be interpreted as His general will for everyone.

We find many examples in the Bible that God is a personal, individual God, who does not act according to a pattern that we have crafted for Him. Personal experiences should not be transformed in theology.

It is not a bad thing to have a personal insight into the Person and work of Jesus, but any personal approach should be based on a firm knowledge of His personality and character outside the shifting context of our life.

My suggestion is that you sit down and make a list of all the things that you believe about God. Make that list for yourself. Write it as though no one will ever see it. If you want to know the Truth, you have to start by being honest with yourself and speaking the truth. Do not "fake" any Christian answers on that piece of paper; God already knows what you believe about Him. My list sounded very much along the lines of: "I felt abandoned by You, I didn't feel loved by You, I didn't feel like I matter to You. I thought You left me, abandoned me and lied to me." That made me realize that I genuinely believed God is a liar; God is unloving; God is indifferent. These lies, brought to the simplest form, were easy to fight against, because I had the Bible to compare this list to. And the Bible tells me the opposite about God.

This list did not scare Him off; He does not take offence and is not intimidated by what people think about Him.

I can assure you if you are brutally honest with yourself and you write down all the lies that you believe about God, you will burst into tears – just as I did. But that list of lies is exactly what you need to pray against: break those lies in the name of Jesus, and you will know that a cloud of confusion has been lifted from your head. Every change God made in my life started in the place of complete vulnerability, honesty and willingness to face the pain of being changed. When you hate the unhealed wounds of your life more than you hate being vulnerable and open towards God, that is when you will give God the opportunity to heal you. Allow the tranquility of God to be mirrored in you.

In other words, if you hurt, run to Christ! And if it feels as if your life is crumbling and your heart is bleeding to death, run to Christ. Never, never, never run away from Him. Your focus is always the Cross, the Son of God and His resurrection. Accept that when you do that, your preconceptions about God – especially the lies – will HAVE to fall because His moving closer to you and your moving closer to Him will bring clarity. He cannot not bring clarity, because He is light. When you run to Him, you have to be ready to face His glory, His immovability and the disfigurement that sin has produced in your life. You will not like yourself – but that is a good thing! Because if you face up to it and cross from the "I love myself" aisle to the "I love Christ" aisle, you will allow Him to rip off all the parts of you that make you ugly and share in His beauty. It will hurt. But it is worth it. It is worth investing your whole self in.

YOUR WIDOWHOOD IS THE LANTERN THAT WILL SHINE LIGHT ON ALL YOUR IDOLS

Before God will do anything in your life, He will present Himself. He will say Who He is. When He does that, surely, without any doubt, any idol will be revealed. God does not share His glory. He does not compromise, and He will never allow His works to be attributed to someone else. We have a jealous God! (Deuteronomy 6:15, Deuteronomy 32:21a, Deuteronomy 32:16, Deuteronomy 5:9, Deuteronomy 4:24, Exodus 20:5)

This should be a massive exclamation mark in any widow's journey: our God is jealous! If anyone worships anything else than Him (be it family, spouse or children), God's wrath will be kindled against them.

God is *very serious* about the idols in our lives. He desires us jealousy for Himself. He is a demanding God, He is not a shy classmate that sends love-notes under the desk. He is a warrior dressed in armor that comes and invites us to follow Him. He is like a man that pursues the woman He loves.

We still do not have an accurate image of God. We still do not understand that any response in our hearts will determine how close He is to us. When in our afflictions we reject Him, even though we might easily and willingly accept a religion in His place, the only One who can heal us takes a step back. But when we call, He answers. His answer and His grace towards us will mean that He will sit next to us and pat us on our shoulder as we waste our time worshiping a dead idol – be it the spouse who died or anything else. I know this is hard to understand, but the most frequent idol in today's society is not a physical statue, it is a person. And often, that person is our spouse. The only way healing is possible, is by agreeing to allow God to put back that person in his or her right place, and then healing can begin.

Do not be fooled: God's intimacy and closeness do not enable us to grieve in ways that are sinful. And His closeness will spread light over many areas of our lives that we did not want to bring into the light.

When you go deeper in your relationship with Christ and you decide to take the risk of moving out of the darkness into His light, He will not only show you how sinful you are inside, He will also show you what your idols are. He will show you what you have invested your life in, instead of investing it in Him. (And no, I am not campaigning for "celibacy means holiness", but there is a God-intended way of making life and family, and there is a man-invented way of doing it.)

YOUR WIDOWHOOD WILL DEMAND A REACTION FROM YOU

James 1:20-24:

"For man's anger does not promote the righteousness God [wishes and requires]. So get rid of all uncleanness and the rampant outgrowth of wickedness, and in a humble (gentle, modest) spirit receive and welcome the Word which implanted and rooted [in your hearts] contains the power to save your souls. But be doers of the Word [obey the message], and not merely listeners to it, betraying yourselves [into deception by reasoning contrary to the Truth]. For if anyone only listens to the Word without obeying it and being a doer of it, he is like a man who looks carefully at his [own] natural face in a mirror; for he thoughtfully observes himself, and then goes off and promptly forgets what he was like."

God cannot heal you unless He comes close to you. And whenever He comes close, His light shines and exposes your sins and your idols. After He sheds light on these things, you can decide to either shut Him out or look for healing in another place, or accept the reality. If, at the beginning, He shows you who He is, He shows you who you are and He shows what you used to run to for comfort, you are left at the crossroads: choose Him and run to Him for comfort, or deny Him and run towards something or someone else.

The problem is that in the face of the reality of death, no idol can stand. Your wounds will not be healed by another human being. Your children cannot heal you; you can pour yourself into child-worshiping and you will accomplish nothing but being hurt even more and hurting your children as well. No idol can satisfy. Self-medicating will destroy you. Ignoring the pain will destroy you. Unless you find healing, you cannot safely enter any new relationships.

Furthermore, you cannot be double-hearted. You cannot run to God and something or someone else in addition to Him. You need to run to God alone, make Him alone responsible for your healing and allow Him alone to heal you. Anything else that you want to add to Him – a relationship, a child, a memory of the lost one – to take you out of your misery will cause you to stumble. You will wake up in the same place, if not worse, after years of torment and unhealed pain.

In the same month when my husband passed away, the husband of one of my connections died. She was about forty-five and I was twenty-five. I met her after three years. Emotionally, she was stuck in the same moment when her husband died. She had not moved one inch from that spot. But the reality is that staying in the same emotional state does not bring back our spouse, parents or children nor does it bring healing. Neither does moving away from it. The only way to be healed to the depths of your heart is not to stay in the same place, nor to move out of it, but to move towards God.

Yes, God will shed light on your heart and you will feel exposed and scared. Yes, you will become vulnerable. But God really is good. He really really really is good and careful with your feelings.

I must warn you that no matter how introverted you are, you will eventually expose your wounds and the thing to which you will expose your wounds will heal or destroy you. There seems to be no exception to this rule. I am very much an introvert, I would never allow myself to disturb anyone with my issues and I would never display my personal problems, even if I risk suffering an implosion. Yet, when my husband died, the pain and the hurt were so strong, and I felt so alone and left without any cover and protection, that I needed to seek someone I could trust, someone who would be willing and able to guide me through the fog of pain I was struggling in. The only Person that I found to be unfailing in their promise to me was Christ. Jesus Christ was the rock that I stood on in the most violent storms I went through. If you choose anyone else than Jesus as the One to guide you and if you take refuge in anyone else, sooner or later that person will surely disappoint you. Family is important, and having a great family is a blessing beyond what our minds can even comprehend; but no parent and no child can heal you when you lose someone you love.

So be strong and courageous. Stand up, shake the dust off and walk on. It is your faith that will make you stronger with every step that you take. Making excuses instead coming to Christ for healing will not actually heal you. And just because you know He could, in theory, heal you, does not mean that you are closer to being healed; but grabbing the edge of His robe, knowing in your heart that you will be healed, will heal you. You cannot sit and let yourself go into wobbliness and emotional paralysis, you need to react. You have to decide to move towards something: either towards Him, or towards what your own mind thinks will bring relief. And time will prove you that even if you decide to stay in the same spot, without taking any action, the people that you love and are still around you will not put their life on hold. They will move on. Your children will grow up and choose partners; and if you are not there for them, as a trusted confident, who will guide them what partners to choose? If you decide to absent yourself from this world and vegetate, you will hurt those around you and you will eventually hurt yourself too. The worst time to stop is when you are hurt.

WHAT WIDOWHOOD IS NOT

YOUR WIDOWHOOD IS NOT AN EXCUSE TO SIN

I will never forget the advice that a so-called Christian woman gave me when hearing Claudiu had died. She said: "Well... you are young... No one expects perfection from you. As long as you are discreet and you do not make a big fuss about it, no one will judge you if you have a one-night stand once in a while. I mean, what can you do? The flesh is flesh and it has his needs... You live alone, don't you? There is no one to see what you do, no one will ever know." I was in utter shock. I looked at her and said nothing. I blinked several times, gave her a stern look of disapproval. I did not know what else to do.

Our pain is not an excuse to sin! Who gave us the right to live in the darkness when we have been made people of light? We need to shine not only when we feel loved, appreciated, and when we have all we want but also when we have nothing because if our holiness is conditioned by a relationship, that holiness is cheap!

In Habakkuk 3:17-19, we read:

"Though the fig tree does not blossom and there is no fruit on the vines, [though] the product of the olive fails and the fields yield no food, though the flock is cut off from the fold and there are no cattle in the stalls, yet I will rejoice in the Lord; I will exult in the [victorious] God of my salvation! The Lord God is my Strength, my personal bravery, and my invincible army; He makes my feet like hinds' feet and will make me to walk [not to stand still in terror, but to walk] and make [spiritual] progress upon my high places [of trouble, suffering, or responsibility]!"

Sin is no lesser a sin if we are hurt when we commit it. The price is still the precious blood of Jesus. We are not allowed to take the Lord's name in vain and make a fool of Him by sinning on purpose, excusing our deeds because of our pain. On the contrary, the last thing that we need in our affliction and pain is to build a wall between us and the only One who can heal us:

"Behold, the Lord's hand is not shortened at all, that it cannot save, nor His ear dull with deafness, that it cannot hear. But your iniquities have made a separation between you and your God, and your sins have hidden His face from you, so that He will not hear. For your hands are defiled with blood and your fingers with iniquity; your lips have spoken lies, your tongue mutters wickedness." (Isaiah 59:1-3)

God is able and willing to save; He can hardly wait to heal us and lift us from our place of pain and suffering. But He cannot help us if we sin because sinning means blocking His ear; it literally means stopping Him from healing us. Never relax your steps while you walk in the holiness that He has placed you in when He sacrificed His Son. Do not ever allow the enemy to teach you that you have an urge that is stronger than the power of the Holy Spirit's prayer for you. If God said that the Holy Spirit prays for us (Romans 8:26-27) and we act as if it were not true, we either call God a liar or we are utterly deceived by the enemy. We have to understand that we stand in Christ not due to our own efforts, but due to the efforts of Christ Himself. And whenever we find ourselves outside Christ it is not because He failed to hold us, but because we placed ourselves there. The truth is that we are not overcome by our desires but we give in to them.

Of course there is grace for those who sin, and the work of Jesus Christ on the Cross assures us of that. But let us not sin simply because grace exists. Do not forget that just because sins can be forgiven, it does not mean that we will not have to deal with the consequences of our decisions. David's sin with Bathsheba was forgiven – yet their first born died. Do not play games with God's holiness and do not forget the promises you made to God. He will honor you when you honor Him in spite of the lure of the world or of your own flesh.

Do not think about sin only in the sense of adultery. Think about it also in terms of financial issues. If your spouse died and left you with unsolved financial problems, do not start stealing from your employer. Do not steal time from your work schedule to spend time mourning. It is honest to take off as much time as needed to recover and to start work again only when you are able to. But do not steal.

Do not lie either. If people ask you how you are and you are not yet fine, say "I trust God." Or something else that is true. No one says that you should pour out all your anxieties and questions on the neighbor that just moved into the flat next door, but do not lie.

The examples can go on. Do not pretend to be someone who you are not and do not follow your flesh. Be who you are and aim that who you are is "Christ in you"; everything else will follow.

YOUR WIDOWHOOD IS NOT AN ILLNESS

It may not necessarily happen, but chances are that some people will treat you as if you were suffering from an illness that can be transmitted over a 100 yards radius from where you are; do not be shocked and do not hate them. They simply have no idea what to say or do. They are powerless in the presence of death; as we all are. The only way they can deal with their own inability to comfort you might be to avoid you. I know it is hard to understand why some people react like this, but if they do, do not blame yourself for their behavior.

You have to accept that there are people who will treat you as if you are ill. They will give you a pretext to prolong your time of mourning. It is healthy to take time to process bereavement and leave the past behind, but the time for healing should not be allowed to delay too long. Accept it; do not feel guilty if you smile. Do not feel guilty if you go to see a film and someone sees you out. This might sound silly for those who have not gone through bereavement, but sometimes even the most common activities like attending church, watching a movie or reading a book can bring guilt on the widowed ones. You are doing nothing wrong if you find something to keep your mind occupied, as long as the activity in itself is not sinful; it is normal to break out of mourning and it is normal to move on. We are all different, so we react differently to pain and we heal in different ways. Even in our bodies, the same knife-cut in the kitchen can heal within various time frames. We are allowed to heal in our own time.

The Bible encourages us to live intentionally, without allowing ourselves to fall into numbness and be tossed about by the winds. The Son of God gave us the power to live with a purpose and gave us the purpose to live for. But at the same time the Bible carefully explains that each season has its own time in Ecclesiastes, chapter 3:

"To everything there is a season, and a time for every matter or purpose under heaven: [...] A time to weep and a time to laugh, a time to mourn and a time to dance."

In painful moments it is important to allow wise and godly people to speak into our lives because ultimately it is God who speaks through the Spirit-filled ones. Do not allow others to rush you into an quick apparent healing, but do not allow those who treat you like an invalid person to enable you to become emotionally and spiritually handicapped. It is not healthy to invest ourselves in relationships in a way that when our partner dies we become depressed or sick with longing. If you detect depression, talk to someone who is led by the Spirit of God and look back into your life up to that point; break off in Jesus's name any unhealthy spiritual bond created between you and the one who has died. Unhealthy spiritual bonds can be created between two living persons and keep on existing after one of them has died. If you do not have anyone close enough to trust them, pray alone. Your prayer is not less effective, but being surrounded by healthy and mature Christians is preferable. If you have not got a spiritual family near you at the time when you lose someone, it might be the right time to start praying that God will bring in your life the right persons to help you in your walk. Listen to what God tells you and go at the pace that He takes you through the process of healing – neither too quickly nor too slowly. Tune yourself to Him, He knows your needs even better than you do.

God held nothing back. God gave us everything He had to the point where He gave not only possessions but who He was. He will not fail you. And if the devil tells you that your God will fail you, you are not to believe him nor allow his lies to make you numb. You are not ill. You are wounded, but wounds do heal. Do not slow down just because everyone expects you to be devastated. Be who Christ made you.

YOUR WIDOWHOOD IS NOT A PROBLEM THAT YOU NEED TO SOLVE

Once everything had settled down after Claudiu's funeral and the families had gone home, I was left alone in the flat where we lived, and I did what any methodical and cerebral person does when facing a problem like death: I defined the problem and I sat down and looked for a solution. I do not think that I have ever heard or read so many unhelpful ideas in my life as I read on the internet in the following weeks. First, I was surprised; but my surprise turned to anger and ended up with amazement as I read all the crazy things people do to get over pain. I realized that emotional healing and losing weight are similar in the sense that there is no recipe but everyone claims to know "the secret".

The only real secret is Jesus. There is no ritualistic habit, no secret prayer, no remembrance celebration, no commemoration, no counting backwards nor imagining that the loved one is near that can heal. All those things are like chasing after the wind.

The reason why we are looking for a recipe for healing is that we need a starting point that we can be utterly convinced that it will not fail us, to use as a foundation to build on.

The stone David was placed on when he cried out to God was Jesus. The stone the Church is built on is Jesus. The foundation of our faith is Jesus's work of sanctification. It is Jesus who gave us the Holy Spirit. And Jesus is the only foundation that we can rely on for healing.

If you ever had any craft activity like cane weaving or sewing, you know that the starting point is the one that makes the difference between a good and a poor piece of work. If you put your faith in anyone else's words other than the Words of God, it is like cutting the first knot and hoping that the netting will be unaltered. It simply does not happen. So do not try to figure out whose advice from what forum is the best. Go back to God and allow Him to guide you. Nobody has a solution for death, but many people are loud and proud. At the end of the day, you cannot blame any decision that you take on anyone's words because the only words that have the consistency required for them to last are God's words. Yes, He speaks through people, but many people speak out of their own wisdom. You need to stay focused on Jesus and your healing will come naturally. Your problem will never be your wound – although it might sound ridiculous. You do not need to find a recipe to heal yourself. You need the doctor: Christ. Stop focusing on your wound, stop being absorbed by the pain, and call the Doctor. Shutting yourself in your room with a deadly wound will not make things better – it will make them worse. You need to have that personal encounter with Jesus to the point where you really trust Him; and if you do trust Him, you will not need to tell Him how to heal you; you just need to follow Him.

YOUR WIDOWHOOD IS NOT A PROOF OF GOD'S LACK OF LOVE TOWARDS YOU

You are not the only one who is challenged by your widowhood and everything that it implies. The new reality challenges your extended family, it challenges your friends and it challenges your children. But most of all, even if you fail to notice or understand it, it challenges God. You might not ever realize, or you might only realize after several years of closely walking with Him, but God never challenges us to *perform* in the circumstances that we walk through. He challenges us to *faith* and *obedience*, but the actual challenge of getting things done is His. He has chosen to challenge Himself on the Cross. And He has taught us that He is worthy of trust to the point where He would die for us rather than fail Himself at being God.

You can never do anything to cause Him to love you more, nor can you do anything to cause Him to love you less. He loves you completely, perfectly, whole-heartedly, from eternity past. He is not looking to gain something out of His relationship with you and He is not there to exploit you. He does not need you; He chooses to share Himself with you because He loves you.

The only death that proves God's love and hate at the same time is the death of Jesus. Jesus died because God loved you perfectly and at the same time He hated sin completely.

Your loved one did not die because God wanted to punish you. S/he did not die because God was caught off guard. S/he did not die because the situation got out of God's control. God does not drop us out of His hand and say: "Oops!"

Yes, as we have seen, there are rare cases in which God decides that enough is enough with one person, but in most cases death is merely a consequence of our living in a sinful and decayed world.

God will never use death as a bogeyman. He simply does not need to do that; He is confident in who He is, so He does not need to resort to frightening us into obedience. He is secure. He can cause us to obey Him without continuously threatening us that He will kill us unless we play the game by His rules; He simply does not do that, it would be a waste of energy if He did. He knows that we know that we are rooted in Him, either we acknowledge it or not. He does not need to treat us like a stern step-father to intimidate us; death is not a blackmail tool in the hands of a megalomaniac, nor is a manipulation tool in the hand of a moody teenager. Death is a law that comes with the existence of sin, as gravity is a law that comes with the existence of a body that floats above the Earth: it is just there! Death was not created for us; we invited it into our world. In other words, it is no more God's fault that we die than it is a bridge's fault that a suicidal person jumps off it. He warned us about the existence of death, He commanded us not to take it in, and we went against His words. Who is there to blame, other than ourselves?

YOUR WIDOWHOOD IS NOT PRIMARILY ABOUT YOU; IT IS PRIMARILY ABOUT JESUS

It took me a long time to understand that my widowhood and my fatherless childhood and my relocation in a foreign country were of great interest to God. We tend to believe that what happens to us individually does not affect people and that it definitely does not matter to God. But the Bible tells us clearly that God listens and hears the cries of widows, and orphans and the cries of foreigners, which is why He made laws to protect them in the Old Testament.

One of the main differences between us and God is the way we relate to events. We see events as isolated; we have a sequential understanding of our lives. And the more we proclaim the development of the independent individual, the less we are interested in the corporate progress of the Body, of the society and the historical succession of events. But we clearly see God is not like this. God is a God who, although personal in having a relationship with us, once we start walking with Him, places us in what He calls "Body of Christ" and makes us aware of His hand at work in the past and His promises for the future. He sees us working together as a unit system, which is why the Spirit sheds light on the uniqueness of each of the system's components by giving us different gifts that enable us to serve each other.

Jesus's death is related to your pain, because He is your brother and He died to eradicate pain. He knows that it is not normal to bury your husband or your child, because He created a world in which these things would have never happened. He knows it is not normal to live as an orphan, because He died to make us His brothers and to make us sons of His Father. He created us as sons, but we went our own way and became enemies, which is why He died to reconcile us with the Father. He came as a foreigner to live among us, so that we would not be strangers to the Father any longer. He took our pain so seriously that He died to stop it.

However, there is a sense in which we do not yet live in the full benefits of His work although His work is accomplished; God is gracious with those that are still not at peace with Him. He found a way of mediating between His wrath and His love on the cross by sacrificing His Son for us. Likewise, He finds a way to mediate between the fullness of the revelation of Christ that will bring an end to funerals and grace for the yet unsaved by giving them time to repent; meanwhile, yes, we live under the consequences of sin and it will cost us, the ones who are saved, our rights to live in a deathless and painless Kingdom that is not yet fully here, although the work that made it possible was completed on the Cross. In this way, we are joining Him in His plan of restoring the creation by giving ourselves as living sacrifices to Him and joyfully accepting that whilst we wait for the Holy Spirit to work in the ones whom He chose, we might lose our spouse or our parents or our children to what we call to be death. We know that they are not dead if they lived in Him, but nevertheless we need to fully accept and understand that following God in His plan comes with a price. I personally accepted that He has not yet stopped all the sin and He still has not come as a Judge, to spare me from the pain of tasting premature death I my family, because He knew that there are others that will taste eternal death if He does not wait for them to repent. So I bowed my head and said: "Yes, Lord, I will follow you even if it costs me everything." – and it cost me nothing less than everything. But I know that I want to be patient with the unsaved and I rejoice that God decided to still give them time to repent. One of the people that I love the most on Earth is still not saved. I want God to be patient with him, and I want him to have time to come to God even if his having time to meet God means that I am stuck in a world where there is death.

God knows that His children are burying their loved ones and that they are hurting. He knows that it is not fair to hurt once we have put our trust in Him, but the paradox is that if He were just with us, even now after we are saved, He would have to cut us off from Himself whenever we sin. If He were to be just with those who are yet unsaved and because of whom sin still has power on Earth, He would probably have to start by cutting off a great percentage of Christians, because we still all sin. God's patience for people's repentance extends, hence, on the church as well. We cannot blame the unsaved for keeping us stuck under the canopy of curse that brings death because we all still commit sin. As long as there is one sin on this Earth, we make ourselves guilty of breaking the entire law, and as long as we break the law we need grace. As long as we need grace, we also need to understand that there is no such thing as "grace for one and not for another"; His grace is for everyone.

You can either trust Jesus and the Father and the Spirit with the timing of the full revelation of Christ, accepting that from the second you are saved till the second you enter His glory you will not be living in a bubble of Paradise but you will suffer the consequences of your sins and those of other people, and either acknowledge or rebel against it. But nevertheless, it is the Father who decides when the time His patience should come to an end and He takes on His Judge's robe. Until then, Christians live in the finished work of Christ, in a world that still is under the effects of sin. Each death matters and each death of the ones that He loves is precious in His eyes. He hurts in our mourning more than we do, because He knows what a deathless world looks like, whereas we do not. Our pain is caused only by our longing for something that we intuitively believe should be different. But He saw His entire creation being trashed and destroyed by the enemy through the hands of the ones He loved. That pain must be greater than ours.

PART THREE

Let The Blood That Is Water Be Water

CHAPTER VII

WAITING ON THE LORD AND WAITING ON OTHERS

Depending on your instinctive reactions, death can bring a greater or lesser degree of panic. But after the initial trauma is over, you will find yourself living in the reality of widowhood. The natural tendency that God blessed us with is that when everything changes around us, we tend to discover in ourselves latent qualities that had not come to light and did not need to manifest themselves up to that point.

This tendency is good, because if we were unable to do that, we could never understand the things that God wants to change in us once our reality starts including Him as Lord and God. The reverse side of the coin is that if you allow the wrong influences into your life particularly at this time of grief, you will be shaped into something hopeless. Bitterness can produce in you either an angry insensitive person that lacks sense or a depressed person that is eaten up inside. Your anger will either be directed to others, or towards yourself, but it will eventually destroy you. If you allow the light of the Word to shine in your life and if you run with your pain to God, He will bring a season of unforeseen closeness to Him – "if we draw near to God, He will draw near us.". That is a promise.

WAITING ON THE LORD

Any other description than what God says about you, is not from Him and will bring bitterness and anger. At the height of the storm, there is no mother, no child, no brother and no pastor that can encounter God in your place. And there is no voice other than His that matters. When death enters so deep into your heart and into your being to the point where it can separate and take the life of the one that you were made one with by God, I think that moment is the closest human experience with what our own mortality will look like: you and God, face to face. That is the moment when He can pour into your heart everything you need to connect with Him to a degree where your relationship with Him will become vital to you. Do not waste this opportunity! It is not often that it happens that you are completely exposed and completely vulnerable in the hand of the Lord; that fresh wound is actually the greatest opportunity to have His Spirit poured into you, because it is not a tiny opening in your heart, but a massive ripping apart.

So do not waste that opportunity of being eternally bound to Him with bonds that cannot be broken, by embracing something that is not eternal – not even if it seems to be religious. Go to God and ask Him to define you. And once you have come through this emotionally traumatic episode in your life, there is an unshakeable ground that you can stand on and catch your breath. That is God's heart for you. God's heart is devastated and He cries every time death ravages His creation and leaves behind a broken heart. How could He not? He is grieved at least as much as you are and He goes through every second of your pain with you, knowing, as He does, your being inside out. If we were aware how painful it is for God to see us hurting, we would melt in fear and trembling and love. God does not classify us by age, gender or race. But the culture you live in, might. Let us go back to the Scriptures and see what is God's heart for us, and then you will be able to clearly distinguish between His voice and the perhaps undefined beliefs that people operate by. But how does God define you?

Depending on the time and culture that you were born in and you are part of, people might have awkward reactions towards widowhood and widows; they might feel uncomfortable in your presence, or will treat you with disdain or with obsequious respect, if your spouse was a public figure. But the truth is widowhood is like a stamp that is placed on you, that is a strong as any other marital status, whether single or married. You will be reminded of it by the everyday bureaucracy, by the old friends and every time someone asks you if you have been married in the past.

People do not know how to react to news about funerals, especially if the ones left behind are really young. When facing really strong emotions, people might feel nervous to the point of bursting into laughter or tears. Do not let that affect you. We are taught that certain circumstances or experiences trigger certain reactions, but actually if the circumstances are extreme, reactions are not predictable. Education and culture works in a relatively safe environment, but when facing a rough reality, that fades and what is left is a naked man in a difficult moment that takes out of him everything he really is and exposes his heart for what it truly is. Yet it is never just your heart that becomes exposed, but the hearts of the ones around you as well. The good news is that the only heart that you need to focus on is God's heart for you. He will deal with the rest.

Do not draw any conclusions about God's heart for you, about His nature or about you, without going back to the Scriptures and going in prayer to Him. Do not allow people to destabilize you in your walk with God. Learn from their reactions, but do not make them into the milestones that you step on. People come and go and so do their words. It is so easy to give advice, and we do that so naturally and sometimes we tell one another the silliest things. And I might add that it is usually those silly ideas that go viral. My challenge for you is that any book that you read, you test and you only take from it what the Holy Spirit tells you to. Submit every word you internalize to the Lord and have Him purify it. He will teach you mouth to mouth everything you need to know about yourself because He loves to teach us. He can hardly wait for us to come to Him and ask Him and talk to Him. He rejoices in our search for Him, and He honors it with His presence. Once you have heard from Him and understood how precious you are to Him and how He sees you, do not allow anything to change or deform the Words that you have received. Test everything through the Scriptures before you embrace it and once you have the certainty that that is the Word of God for you, do not let it go. In the midst of your pain and anxiety, if you look to Jesus with all your heart, He has promised that He will answer. Exodus chapter 22 verses 22-24:

"You will not take advantage of the widow or the fatherless. If you do and they cry out to me, I will certainly hear their cry. My anger will be aroused, and I will kill you with the sword; your wives will become widows and your children fatherless." – the NIV version and the New American Standard Bible: ""You shall not afflict any widow or orphan. "If you afflict him at all, and if he does cry out to Me, I will surely hear his cry; and My anger will be kindled, and I will kill you with the sword, and your wives shall become widows and your children fatherless."

Can you honestly imagine any greater warranty of protection over you than God telling someone: "If you harm her or her children, I will kill you."? Whoever harms you will be killed. Whoever harms your orphan children, will be killed. It is God saying that.

You might see this not as a great patch of spiritual ground on which you can start building on, but it is enough for you to kneel, and it has been tested for generations. It is solid. It is God's Word and therefore enough for you to stand on and start working out your relationship with God from that point. Even if you think you are a great Christian, widowhood will humble you in ways that can be either disastrous and painful or fruitful and enlightening in understanding Who God is and who you are in Him.

EXPECT GOD TO IDENTIFY WITH YOU EMOTIONALLY, TO UNDERSTAND AND PROTECT YOU

Every time I read the Scriptures and I go back to the verses that speak about widows and God's heart for them, I feel dearly loved. Read with me the following verses:

Deuteronomy 27:19: "Cursed is anyone who withholds justice from the foreigner, the fatherless or the widow."

Psalms 68:5: "A father to the fatherless, a defender of widows, is God in His holy dwelling."

Deuteronomy 10:18: "He defends the cause of the fatherless and the widow, and loves the foreigner residing among you, giving them food and clothing."

Psalms 146:9: "The Lord watches over the foreigner and sustains the fatherless and the widow, but He frustrates the ways of the wicked."

Proverbs 15:25: "The Lord tears down the house of the proud, but he sets the widow's boundary stones in place."

Jeremiah 49:11: ""Leave your orphans behind, I will keep them alive; and let your widows trust in Me."

One of the accusations that God brings against Israel in the passage from Ezekiel 22 called "Judgment on Jerusalem's sins" is in verse 7:

"In you they have treated father and mother with contempt; in you they have oppressed the foreigner and mistreated the fatherless and the widow."

God takes our afflictions and our pain very seriously, and He will fight anyone who fights against the ones that are afflicted and defenseless.

For a long time I did not understand for a long time how the rule of "He went through every single kind of suffering that you could ever experience", that Christians seem to deduce from Hebrews 4:15 can apply to widows, orphans or foreigners. I always thought that was just a way of using words to trigger butterfly feelings when we think about Jesus. But the question about the content of His cup of suffering lingered in my heart: if He was never in love, if He was never a groom losing His bride, how can He understand my pain? And how can He have tasted my widowhood, so that He could identify with my emotions and my anxiety? – If He did not, can I *really* trust Him?

But the truth is, the reason why God has such a determined heart to defend the widows, the orphans and the foreigners is precisely the fact that Jesus Himself was the first widow in the history of heavens and earth. That is why God's anger can be kindled to the degree of Him promising to kill the ones that afflict widows: His Son died for the suicidal Bride. Jesus was the abandoned Son of God and He was the alien High Priest and King dwelling among us. He definitely tasted widowhood, abandonment and alienation.

I believe this is a perspective that we do not often picture God in, but when Adam and Eve betrayed God and decided to entrust the authority over their land and life to the enemy (by trusting his words rather that God's), they literally committed spiritual suicide. The act of casting out of the Garden of Eden was God conducting the funeral of the suicidal bride of Christ. And Christ decided that rather than living forever in the awareness that His bride foolishly cheated Him to her own death, He would come and die the death she deserved. (I want to underline the fact that the theological debate if it is accurate to call it that, as to whether before the coming of Christ the chosen people were part of the Bride is a non-topic with regard to the pain God himself felt when the human beings that He created misused the free will they were given, deciding to kill themselves.) The truth that emerges is that Adam and Eve chose death over God and, as a result, died.

There are numerous references in the Bible where God keeps promising blessings to those who bless His chosen people that after Christ's coming were called "the Bride". And there are terrible generational curses cast over those afflicting her; Christ has an untamed passionate heart for her, He loves His bride to death - literally.

When Jesus is asked about His disciples not fasting as the Pharisees did, Jesus simply says (Matthew, chapter 9 v.14, 15):

"Then John's disciples came and asked him, "How is it that we and the Pharisees fast often, but your disciples you will fast?" Jesus answered, "How can the guests of the bridegroom mourn while he is with them? The time will come when the bridegroom will be taken from them; then they will fast."

Jesus saw Himself as a bridegroom. Jesus knew His mission was to bring His suicidal Bride back into life, back where she belonged, in unity with Him. Jesus has had the heart of a widow: but during His rescue mission, He did not have emotional outbursts and depressions.

He trusted the Father, and drew near to Him. This is how He identified with us in our widowhood – likewise, we need to identify with Him in our widowhood and learn from Him how to allow our widowhood to be fruitful by drawing near to the Father.

The pain that God experienced when casting out human beings from the Garden of Eden was real and intense; the pinnacle of His creation, the apple of His eye, the Bride, His children, His friends, His image died. That is not an easy funeral to attend.

The 54th chapter of the book of Isaiah has been for years a solid ground for me to stand on because the way in which God speaks to the Israelites proves the fact that He has an intimate knowledge of the anxiety and distress that the people were going through. But the fact that He has chosen to make a parallel between their pain and a widow's pain is amazing, because He obviously knows what widowhood feels like. This is why He brings the two images together: the imagery of the deserted nation and that of a widowed wife:

"The Lord will call you back as if you were a wife deserted and distressed in spirit — a wife who married young, only to be rejected," says your God. For a brief moment I abandoned you, but with deep compassion I will bring you back. In a surge of anger I hid my face from you for a moment, but with everlasting kindness I will have compassion on you," says the Lord your Redeemer." (verses 6-8).

EXPECT GOD TO EXPECT YOU TO COME TO HIM

In the previous chapter, we looked at what widowhood is not, and one of the key aspects of how we should go through widowhood is that whatever afflicts us, we need to run to the Father. This is not only true of widowhood; but of any pain that we might endure. Any time something hurts, we need to go to what comforts us, and if that is not the Father, it clearly means that we have idols. God actually expects us to run to Him. He calls us to Him repeatedly –

"Come to Me, all you who labor and are heavy-laden and overburdened, and I will cause you to rest. [I will ease and relieve and refresh your souls.]" (Matthew 11:28)

Jesus speaks about salvation over Jerusalem, cries, and says:

"If only you would have known... at least today..." (Luke 19:42)

Going to God does not mean something sophisticated, like making oaths, countless prayers, struggling with doing good, checking a list of requirements. Going to God means kneeling and being honest with Him. It really is that simple: stop running. God does not withhold His peace from us. He does not place conditions on His presence in our lives; He wants to be present in our lives. But no matter what He does, He cannot be present unless we want Him in our lives. In any relationship both parties must want to be with each other, otherwise it is not a relationship, it is like taking hostages.

EXPECT GOD TO EXPECT YOU TO BE HOLY

God wants to be in our lives, but He cannot accommodate with our sinful lives. You might wonder why I keep talking about sins and effects of sins in a book aimed at widows, but widowhood does not make us holy by default. And when we are afflicted, we might feel that we have the right to be a little bit more relaxed – when in fact, that is the most important moment to walk with God and not allow ourselves to be separated from Him by sin!

Part of God's Fatherhood responsibilities towards His children is that He corrects us and He brings us back. Being aware that you placed God in the wrong place in your life, because you placed the one who has died before Him does not mean you are judged and condemned – it means God loves you and wants to point out something that you were doing wrong so He would be able to bring you back under His authority. When you are under His authority, He can bless you. When God points our sins to us, He is acting out of grace, mercy and goodness. He does not rebuke you, He tells you what to let go of because He sees better than you whatever you have and hold in your hands as lord and god instead of Him. He wants to manifest Himself as your Defender, but He cannot do so as long as you do not stay under His dominion. Do not feel rejected, but feel loved, deeply loved.

EXPECT GOD TO EXPECT YOU TO BELIEVE HIS WORD AND TO BE AVAILABLE FOR HIM EVEN IF YOU DO NOT "FEEL LIKE IT"

God understands us and we have grace in our walk with Him, but He wants us to start believing what He tells us through Scriptures or through His words. He wants us to develop a spiritual stature in time and we need to grow. He expects us to feed on His Word and to listen to what He says, especially in times of testing. How can He guide us if we do not listen? We expect our children to trust us, to communicate with us and to listen to what we tell them; why do we not trust God? Is He not trustworthy?

Our communication with Him and our obedience to Him cannot be conditioned by what happens to us or around us. On the contrary, what happens to us and around us needs to be seen through the relationship that we have with Him. There is no other way to live in holiness other than actually living in holiness. He is our compass and our guide, not circumstances and events.

EXPECT GOD TO USE YOU IN THE LIVES OF OTHER CHRISTIANS

Expect Him to bring across your path many people as hurt as you are and expect Him to use your suffering in the long term. If your pain really has been fruitful, you will know that, because there will be many who will come to rest in the shadow of your branches and eat from the fruit that you bear. Expect God to make the most of your obedience, and to work through you. And be willing to serve when He does so.

Elijah was fed by a widow. Jesus was blessed in the Temple by Anna, a prophet's widow. Jesus used as an example the action of a widow who gave her last two coins for the temple. God will surely use your weakness and He will use your inability to bring forth something that lasts forever. God is interested in eternity, not in things that come and go. When you give away your last piece of bread, you do not merely give out a slice of bread; you actually give out everything that you have. I have experienced God's goodness in that precise way. And there were times when He asked me to give the last coin I had, literally. I did, and He never failed to provide for me. He started asking for more, and more, till I was completely detached from the stuff that I had because in time my heart became attached to things that cannot be seen but last forever (Luke 12).

WAITING ON OTHERS

As important as it is to wait on the Lord to get involved in your life, it is of equal importance to know that salvation does not just come from the Lord, it comes *only* from the Lord.

I will repeat what I said in the previous chapter, because we need to take hold of this truth: *we were not created to die, so death scares us. We do not know how to react when we face death, and we do not know how to react when someone we love dies.* So do not expect people's reactions to you to be perfect, completely supportive, just and mature. After Claudiu died, I was sure that I would know how to react when someone I love lost a close relative, and I soon discovered that I still do not know how to react because each death bears within it a proof of our limitations and deceit. If your family is supportive, hears what you say and has healthy boundaries, it is rather more useful if you articulated exactly what your needs are at that time. If you are an introvert or your family is not supportive (or is completely absent), please do not expect the world to stop for you and to love you. Remember, you run to God for comfort and love, not to people. The well-intentioned ones (and there are a lot of well-intentioned people out there!) will make a great difference in the way you move out from the place of mourning, but if there is no one around you who cares, remember that God cares and that that is everything that you need to move on. And be very careful to predators – there are *many* out there wearing sheep clothing.

WHAT TO EXPECT FROM THE CHURCH

Do not expect perfection. One of the shocks I had was that in the church I attended during my time of mourning, I became a topic of debate as to whether I was a true widow or not (due to my age and the age stated in Bible to "qualify" as a widow – although that is a typical misunderstanding of the spirit in which the 1 Timothy 5 passage was written), whether I would be allowed or not to wear white in church if I ever got married again, and all kinds of nonsense. Looking back, I find it really funny, because in my practical walk with Jesus, none of these things made any difference especially since my wounded heart was not exactly drawing me near to any bridal shop. But when I was in that frame of mind, I felt as if I was being punished by the community for losing my husband, which made no sense to me. I wasn't even considering getting married again at that point and to this day, I have no idea how that entire debate started.

I know my position towards the church is difficult to understand. I love the church. There has been nothing that hurt me more than the church. Yet, I love it, because Christ, My Glorious Boaz, He loves it. So please, if it is in any way possible, be kind to the church, even if under pressure, the church will not be nice to you. If they forget that we are all on a journey, you can decide yourself to not forget that we are all on a journey; no one has the full revelation of Christ yet, but everyone is quite opinionated and the journey is not a silent one. Kids!

The definition of widowhood has changed over years, and frankly in today's culture, we do not have too many words that have kept their original meaning. There have been linguistic changes and cultural influences all over the world. When everything around you changes, the last thing you want is to stand on shifting sands. But the good news is that you do not stand on what people think or say about the context you are in from outside. You stand on what God tells you. You stand on Jesus, and He is a safe rock to build upon. Your faith is not in people, and your help does not come *from* people, although it may come *through* people. Your salvation, your justification, your Truth is Jesus.

I know that it is not the best time to learn how to keep yourself away from all the gossip that goes on, from all the comments and remarks, but if you learn in this painful period how to walk in holiness with your God in spite of the circumstances and in spite of your entire world collapsing around you, you will learn something that is worth more than decades of day and night theological study: you learn God's heart. You learn His compassion for the people who behave stupidly around you and you learn to give grace out of His grace, not out of your own resources. (At this point, you have no other resources.) You learn not to judge them and you learn how to pray effectively, not against people but against the spirits that trigger a ridiculous reaction. Your spiritual insight can develop within a few days more than it otherwise would in decades. This is all possible because when you are in that place, if you choose to cling to God and only to God, you will feel as if you are thrown into a pressure cooker to wrestle with the Spirit of God. And something will happen: your flesh will die. From that point on, God can use you to turn the world upside down, because you reached a point of complete trust and abandonment into the hands of the God whom you trust and love. And that is why it is important to stay under His hand; yes, it will hurt – it will hurt terribly! – but He is good and He will bring forth through you the unique flavor of love. There is nothing else in this world that is worth dying for, other than allowing Him to work through you in other people's lives. And if the people that He wants to work in are those who should support you but fail to do so, He will support you and make you a beam of light for them. Remember, He loves them as well, just as much He loves you.

Expect those around you to look at you through the lens of widowhood and to label you, but do not allow that to shape your identity. Your identity is still Christ in you, not "the widowed one". Yes, experiences that we go through might explain who we are, but they do not determine who we are, they do not put a definition on us and they cannot limit us.

Another thing which is very likely to happen is that your brothers will feel awkward in your presence. They do not know how to relate to you in your pain. Look at Job's friends – they were all well intended but none of them understood the complexity and the dimension of Job's pain. They did not know any better than to try to justify God and to play God's advocates, hence to blame Job for his pain. But you have a great ally in the Spirit of God, and He goes before you. He surrounds you. He talks to you and He guides you. You are to follow Him, not other voices. You will hear so much bad advice and so many temptations will come down your path; follow only God's Word.

When David was out in the fields, looking after the sheep, no one was there with him. It is there that he learned how to kill lions – it was either him or the lion that had to go down and David decided that his life was precious. At the end of the day, it does not matter who is with you in your trials or who is not there, it matters who is *in* you. If there is a spark of life in you that flows out from God's presence, that twinkle of life is enough to ignite you back into living in spite of having to go through the valley of the shadow of death.

WHAT TO EXPECT FROM THE DEVIL

The devil cannot harm us, if we are children of the Lord. But he will try to intimidate us and will explore any single circumstance that he can detect to drag us in a state of insecurity or numbness.

Expect him to lie. The devil lies a lot and has a deceiving nature. The way you discern between truth and lies is by being deeply rooted in God's Word. In one of the previous chapters we have looked at some of the lies that the devil invents to bring us into spiritual paralysis. This is not a complete list, he will fabricate whatever he needs to, in order to cut us off from the Father. If we feel defeated by him and misled by God, he wins. His purpose is always to break our relationship with the Father, which is why he will invent lies and he will hit either in what we believe about Jesus or in what we believe about the completed work of Christ. If he can separate us from the Father, he is in full control.

The devil knows no shame. He will not spare you from his activity because you are hurt, on the contrary: the more you are in pain, the more vulnerable you are, and the more He will be on your tail. That is why it is so important to be quick and intentional in your healing. God is with us in the valley of the shadow of death as we *pass* through it, not as we decide to have a picnic in it or even build our houses there. Do not camp in the valley. Do not stay in the place of vulnerability any longer than you have to, but do not, on the other hand, lie to yourself saying that everything is all right. Everything is *not* all right, so walk away towards a place of spiritual security.

The enemy has no sense of remorse and he will never refrain from doing us harm. One of the tactics he uses to harm us is to pay attention to the lies that we believe about ourselves and asserting them to be true. The reason why he can get us to give credence to a lie is because we already have a preconceived idea and he uses the pattern of our thinking to point towards something that is false. For instance, if a young mother thinks of herself as a failure as a mother, if her child hurts himself in the playground as she watches closely over him, she will think: "Oh, I am a terrible mother because my son hurt himself.", when the reality is that her child got hurt because that is what young children do as they discover the environment. It is just a normal process of learning, not a proof of her inability. That thought does not come from the Spirit of God, it is condemnatory not convicting, and it brings anxiety and depression, not a healthy emotional reaction. But the one responsible for accepting that thought to bear fruit is the mother. Remember, if we humble ourselves under God and resist the devil, he will flee from us.

Reject the devil. Make no compromise with him. He is evil and intentional in his evilness. Expect him to overload you with what you fear the most if you make any compromise with him. Expect him to bring the wrong people, especially the wrong men or women into your life after the death of your spouse has died. If you truly believe that you need a relationship with another human being to be complete and you look for a relationship to fulfill you, he will bring unsuitable people across your path to give you what you want, but take away your peace and your relationship with the Father.

Expect him to hang out a lot around you and attempt to undermine your physical life and health. He knows you are hurt. The wounded are the most vulnerable. He is not stupid, he is evil and cunning and this combination will be fatal if you wander away from the track. Vultures gather over a corpse. Allow God's love to resurrect you from mourning and do not allow yourself to become the one that runs away from the devil, but the one that the devil flees away from. Yes, it is possible. Jesus gave us this authority and this power, and Jesus's work is not limited by our context. He gave you the power to overcome the devil not only when you are happy and life is good. He gave you the power to overcome the devil at all times. In fact, the devil is chasing you because he knows that if you realized the power Jesus gave you over him, you would become a huge inconvenience. You can, in prayer, take apart his kingdom brick by brick. So he would rather hunt you down while you are numb with pain, rather than face you when you stand bold. See how cowardly he is?

Having a general idea about the devil's work is important not because we have to start looking for signs of his presence everywhere. That would be living in fear. We are not to focus on the devil, but on Christ. Yet we should acknowledge that our emotional healing is of worth and that the devil will fight to throw us into addictions or troubled ungodly relationships to prevent that healing.

One of my friends lost her husband and out of nowhere all these weird non-Christian guys appeared. It was not just one guy; it was a long chain of them. She never dated any of them, but they were hunting her down like jackals. She told me how every time one of them appeared, although some of them seemed to be nice and understanding and had some ideas of salvation, the Holy Spirit would tell her one word about that man, and she would know that he is not from Him. About one man, He told her: "He is a violent man." So she told him not to call her any more. His reaction was: "Ha! Let me see how that God of yours will give you a man to marry!" Later on, she learned from third parties that the reason why his former wife divorced him was because he was abusive. My friend is about to marry a wonderful Christian minister.

God really *can* be trusted with step-by-step guidance. He really does share His secrets and His hidden things with the ones who trust and confide in Him. He knows the deepest secrets of one's heart and He guides and protects those who seek Him first.

WHAT TO EXPECT FROM FAMILY AND FRIENDS

It is not uncommon for the family of the surviving partner to be utterly confused and unable to cope with the reality. Understanding what the surviving partner goes through, understanding the emotions, the practical aspects of the new reality and figuring out the perfect way to help the wounded is quite difficult for anyone. Underlying this perplexity is a thick layer of personal unresolved emotions and questions, which can sometimes hinder any rational response. Pain is never easy to deal with.

Suppressed anger is one of the most common reactions; and sometimes, the anger that the family of the widowed carries is greater than that of the one who was widowed. The feelings of those around the widowed are as legitimate and as real as those of the widowed. Especially when the age of death was untimely or the circumstances of the death were not natural, all those who knew the dead person will be affected.

We were created with the capacity to feel sorry, to feel sympathy, to identify with the pain of the ones we care for. We have an entire pop industry based on the ability to identify with the experiences of those presented as role-models. Teenagers cry over love songs they identify with, young adults get angry over the injustice they see on news reports, mothers cringe when they hear of child abuse. Those who grow up as orphans will have a stronger reaction when they will meet other orphans – they will either love them more than others, or else ignore them completely because they need to deny what happened in their past.

You have to understand that you are not the only one hurting and suffering, but all those around you. One of the greatest pains that I have ever experienced was seeing my younger brother being raised without a dad. To this day, although he is an amazing man and is married to a wonderful woman, I still know that he was robbed of something that should have been his, something that he would never get back – a childhood with his father. His pain of lacking memories with our father hurts me more than it hurt not to have a daddy to take me down the aisle on my wedding day; my father was the father of both of us, and it hurts for me, but it also hurts me for my brothers and for my mother to have lost him.

You might have to face denial. Some people simply cannot cope with the reality, so they deny what happened and act as if nothing happened. If someone uses plural when they talk to you, including your dead partner in the "you", do not assume that the person is unaware or muddle headed. At a subconscious level s/he still denies what happened; s/he has no bad intentions towards you, but needs time to adjust to reality. S/he might be numb with pain and sadly, they might be mourning even years later.

You might face the desire for extreme, suffocating closure coming especially from those who were supposed to be in authority over you before your spouse came on the scene of your life. Especially parents and tutors or elder brothers might feel that they should have protected you from the great harm of losing the one you loved, to the point of feeling real guilt and failure. They are not responsible for your widowhood, of course, but until the waters clear, they might look through the muddy waves and see something that it is not there. Or, experiencing the same false-guilt feelings, they might push you away in the attempt to get away from the pain. You might remind them so much of the pain and trauma that they have experienced, that they will just ignore and avoid you.

There is, of course, a good way in which parental protection can manifest itself even if you are in mature adulthood, when your spouse died. The reason the Law required the widowed to return to their parents' house was for protection and comfort. But the motivation underlying that specific Law was to ensure that the woman was placed under protection and authority. We know now that the Church is our extended family, so if your natural family happens not to be physically around you, make sure you stay under healthy, godly authority and protection. Stay safe. In order to find healing, you need to be safe. If you have to constantly watch your back and protect yourself actively, like a sheep among wolves, you will not be able to allow God heal you because you will be busy fighting off disturbances. Make sure you place yourself in the safest social environment possible, and try to get involved in a healthy church community. Both extreme closeness to family and friends and extreme detachment can cause anxiety and can delay healing for both you and your children.

However your family reacts, try to be patient. It is a painful time for everyone. No one is able to fully control their emotions in times like these. If there were any issues unresolved between you and the family of the one who died (everyone knows in-laws can be a sensitive issue!), it is most likely that problems will resurface at this point. When you cannot cope with their reactions, go in your room and pray. And your Father who is in heaven will hear you and will strengthen your feet. But never forget to make no compromise when it comes to your safety and that of your children.

Do not expect your family or your friends to take away your pain; they are simply unable to do so. Do not expect them to know how to react. Do not expect them to be perfect – no one is perfect.

Make sure the friends you and your spouse had before as common friends are not turning into predators, especially if you are a woman. There is an interesting natural law that God placed in men, that they are to protect women. And there's something about divorced and widowed women, something that makes men feel the need to step up and take the place of the one who left. If these men were godly, everything would be perfect. But most of them are not; they just see an easy prey and gather around it. ("The Luring Waters" chapter develops this topic.)

Your children's reaction to their parent's death can also be unexpected. There is a good chance that they will wonder if it is their fault that their parent has died. Children have an unlimited creativity resource when it comes to finding reasons why they are to hold themselves guilty for the death of their parents. Also, you will notice that their sense of justice will increase significantly, because in their hearts they know that it is not right just to bury their parent when they needed parenting the most. So any injustice at school, with friends, among siblings, may trigger a reaction that seems to be disproportionate if they are not taught how to deal with their loss in a healthy way. Do not forget, it is not only your spouse but also their parent who died, so there *has* to be room for their pain to be expressed as well.

As an orphan I always found myself wondering if I had not been an orphan, whether trivial everyday things would have happened if my dad had still been around. If someone jumped the line right in front of me, I would wonder: "If I still had a dad, would this person still jump the queue line in front of me?" or if someone addressed me in an aggressive tone, I would wonder if they would have had the same tone if my father had been alive. In spite of knowing in my child-like mind that these things have nothing to do with my father and that the persons who were sinning against me had no idea that I don't have a father, in my heart I felt a deep need at least to ask myself those questions. My mind would always kick in and explain to myself again that no one knew if my father was alive or not, hence it could not possibly have anything to do with it. In my post-teen, early young adult years, I became afraid to express these questions to myself because I was wondering if it was normal to ask myself if these random events were connected to my father's death. Later on I met Jesus and my questions have changed, but looking back, all I can say is that I was a healthy child, emotionally and intellectually, and I was needed to get over this pain, so I had to swim through all the contradictions and paradoxes. And you cannot swim without getting wet.

I still miss my father, to this day. It has been over fifteen years since he died and although since his death I have buried grandparents, uncles and even my husband, my father's death is still there, and no matter how many years pass and how deep the healing goes, I still think about him and I still have moments when

I miss him terribly. Not because I *need* him, but because I loved him to bits and I miss his company. I miss holding hands with my dad and I miss his humor.

Having grown up as an orphan is an experience that does not self-delete from your mind when you reach adulthood; and widowhood does not un-happen when you remarry or decide to stay single. Those experiences are still there even if there is a transfer of responsibilities when a widow marries, and a new line of authority comes in with the new husband. We cannot erase them. But we can choose to see God's goodness and His faithfulness through these experiences. Respect your children's right to walk their walk with God – do not expect them to know how to deal with their emotions, do not expect them to get it right. They will not get it right from the word "go", you need to educate them and not abandon them in this maze of sorrow. They are as much in pain as you are, as devastated as you are. Do not suffocate them, do not neglect them, do not allow others to suffocate them or to cause them pain and do not place yourself in a place where there is no safety for them because when they become adults, they will know that you placed something else above them. It is not a matter of shame to look for professional advice on how to help them transition safely through the season. It doesn't mean that you are unable as a parent to raise up children: it only means you as a family have suffered a great loss and you need support.

WHAT TO EXPECT FROM YOURSELF

Expect yourself to have an "I have lost the direction of my life!" feeling. That is exactly what happens: your life will no longer follow the same pattern. There are new challenges ahead and there are things that you will stop doing, and things you will start doing. Your life will never be the same, but that does not necessarily mean that, in the long run, it will be worse. It simply means "different". Whether your life is different in a good or bad way is up to you. You have the power to decide and the strength to make it happen – but if you do nothing, nothing will happen.

Expect yourself to have a reaction towards God. There is no way death will not trigger any reaction towards the god you believe in, and if you are a Christian, you will have something to ask or something to tell God. You might feel anger towards God. Like David, you might feel offended and confused. If your first reaction is to be angry, God is big enough to take your anger, your questions and your struggles. Talk to Him. I have seen so many examples of angry persons in the Bible, who took all their perplexity to God. He never rebuked them if they were honest and were honestly looking to meet Him. Do not lie; do not pretend to be strong when you are not, especially not in prayer. Do not assume you must be weak just because you have never been in this situation before. He gives you the anointing to carry your cross once you get it. And He has forgiven you even before you got upset with Him. Do not blame Him for your pain – just come with the wound, as ugly and as painful as it may be, and He will clean it.

Expect yourself to start hating the idea of marriage, due to fighting the fear of burying the new partner like you did the first; this fear can increase in time to the point of not entering into any new relationship or stepping out of a happy one. This does not prove that you are ill-intended towards the new partner, it simply means that you are afraid and where fear is allowed to nest for years, love has to crack a hard shell. This is why you might be inclined to choose short-term (and potentially destructive) relationships over stable ones. The idea of loving again and become vulnerable in the face of death can only be tamed and reduced to the right size by Jesus's perfect love and the resurrection power that we have in Him.

Expect yourself to feel pressured to be perfect – even if no one is applying any real pressure. If it seems to you that everyone is studying your reactions, the reality is that some do watch, some don't; you might disagree, but the truth is, it is not your problem if anyone watches you, unless you make it a problem. Having to deal with one funeral does not make you perfect overnight and it does not give you any special "master-mourner" accreditation. The "no one's perfect" rule applies in widowhood. You are allowed not to be perfect; you are allowed to be human. You are not allowed to sin, but you are allowed to feel vulnerable and you do not need to pretend to be in any way different from what you are. God already knows who you are and He loves the way He created you – otherwise, He would have simply made you in a different way! (Psalm 139:1-4).

Do not hate yourself if you have no answers. Do not hate yourself if you struggle. But let your struggling be hopeful, not self-destroying. Jesus gave you hope and 1 Corinthians 15:54b-58 clearly says it:

"Death is swallowed up (utterly vanquished forever) in and unto victory. O death, where is your victory? O death, where is your sting? Now sin is the sting of death, and sin exercises its power [upon the soul] through [the abuse of] the Law. But thanks be to God, Who gives us the victory [making us conquerors] through our Lord Jesus Christ. Therefore, my beloved brethren, be firm (steadfast), immovable, always abounding in the work of the Lord [always being superior, excelling, doing more than enough in the service of the Lord], knowing and being continually aware that your labor in the Lord is not futile [it is never wasted or to no purpose]."

CHAPTER VIII

THE LURING WATERS

One of the first things that you will find out if you study the history of warfare is that there are two types of attack in a battle. War strategies are fascinating and they reveal what is happening in the spiritual world. The first type counts on the surprise factor as being decisive in winning the battle and the second one relies on wearing down the resistance of the opponent over time. The first one relies on the sharpness and intensity of the attack, the second one on perseverance and longevity of the attack.

I have learned about fortresses and combats while studying architecture; architects had to develop designs that would be effective in resisting the enemy regardless of the battle strategy that he chose. The architecture of citadels was very much shaped by the operating range of the weapons used in specific periods of time and the designs had to evolve as the armaments industry developed new weapons. Architects had to work on perfecting wall angles, window sill shapes and the access area. A fortress is static, so it cannot defend itself by attacking the enemy. The enemy comes to steal and destroy and the only way that a fortress can stay intact is if the watchmen can see the danger from afar, the people inside are well prepared and the architecture itself is designed in such a way that it allows the people trapped inside to cover a good range from afar when the enemy approaches. (The topic is extremely interesting – these few lines are merely a short reference to the science of engineering, that took centuries to perfect.)

As the Body of Christ we are defined as "living stones", which means that we have another option than only to wait for the enemy to come close and hope we are strong enough to endure the attack; unlike a static citadel, we are "alive". But we are human and there are times in which the emotional charge and the psychological load that we carry are so intense that we simply cannot react in a pro-active way. At those times, Jesus promises that He is our tower of refuge. But the tower of refuge is of no use if the watchers which should defend the city are allowing the enemy in.

It is not only defense architecture design that was conceived in the spirit of what efficient defense during a time of war means. If you look at war machines, war ships – and basically the whole armaments industry in modern times, they all indicate that there is a type of attack that is short and sharp and a type of attack that is slow but persistent.

We, the human race, did not invent war. But we find ourselves in a battle, having joined the wrong side. The good news is that the victory already is assured in Christ. What that does not mean is that the devil will shrink back from trying to make us think that we are at the end of our strength and give up. We are not facing any war in our own strength and the outcome of the battle has already been reached and revealed but if we believe when the devil tells us that we are alone and defeated, then in our perception, the outcome is yet to be decided. The natural reaction we will have is to grab onto "something firm" to survive, and that something will probably not be Jesus.

I used to read Psalm 139 as being one of the Psalms in which David analyzes his options when he wanders where could he go where God is not present (v.7-12). But what he is actually saying is that there is nothing that can hide him from God's care and watchfulness. David knows that darkness does not prevent God's loving eyes from seeing him. He knows that the depths of the sea are not deep enough to separate him from God. The night is as clear as the day to the Lord and nothing will stop God's fierce love from enfolding him. That is a truth that we all need to get hold of because when we understand that there is nothing that can separate us from

God, we cease to be afraid of life's circumstances or trials. No matter how deep the seas in which life tosses us, God's loving eyes can see through the waters and He will not allow one hair to be touched. And that unstoppable love is the *only* solid ground to build on – not a new relationship or an addiction. We are not a people who look to people for salvation. We are a people who have a God that will go through walls if He needs to, to catch us. He is what our security stands on, not a relationship. During testing times, He stands when all else fails. During widowhood, He stands. You do not need to substitute Him with a relationship. You do not need other ground to stand on – you already have the ground to stand on. Rise, take up your bed and walk!

The two main dangers that a newly widowed person is exposed to is either to choose a non-Christian partner who admits to being a non-Christian, or to step into a wrong relationship with a long-time church attender who is not born again. We will look at both cases and I pray that if you find that you have already made the mistake of entering into a relationship with the wrong person, you will not feel condemned but that you will understand the seriousness of the situation you are in and that you will seek help from a mature Christian pastor. If you recognize that you are about to make either of these wrong choices, please stop and pray and allow the Holy Spirit to guide you.

WHAT A CHRISTIAN BELIEVES ABOUT MARRIAGE

In one of the previous chapters we looked at what marriage means from a biblical perspective. Let us review briefly what the Bible says about marriage.

The born-again Christian will relate to others as God relates to him. The unsaved learn from their physical parents how to relate to others, but born-again Christians inherit God's heart as the Ideal Servant of God – the Son of God – is reproduced in them. The heart of the Son of God takes shape in them as they allow themselves to be adopted into God's family through the work of the Spirit.

This being the case, we all face disappointments in relationships, which usually lead to either a fight between the partners or abandonment. We all sin and we know no other way to react to sin than to either abandon the sinner or to fight with him hoping that if we nag him enough we will educate him/her into behaving in a way that does not trigger animosity between the two partners. But neither of these two ways of dealing with sin in a relationship (whether committed by us or against us) actually work – hence the increasing number of divorces. The only real hope for a lifelong authentic relationship in which there is mutual whole-hearted commitment is that when we are caught in a perfect relationship with a perfect companion (Jesus Christ) we learn from Him that there is another possible reaction to sin, and that is covenant. God's reaction to our sin was neither to kill us all nor to abandon us, but He whole-heartedly committed Himself to us to the point of sacrificing Himself for us and establishing a way for us to approach Him in spite of the fact that His presence, outside His grace, would consume us.

At the same time, remember that the devil is cruel and presumptuous. He is real and he fights fiercely against us. One of the most successful tactics that the devil uses against the wounded is to keep trampling on the wound, preventing the healing. If he cannot wound you, he will use any painful circumstance of your life to stir pain. Anything that will keep you focused on anything other than Christ will be certainly used against you or anyone – pain, pride, loss, depression, addictions. It is vital for us to know that although the battle is won and we are victorious in Christ, we cannot expect anyone else to walk in victory in our place – we need to grasp it and hold it and to walk in it by ourselves. Christ's victory is the gateway, the breakthrough that He made in the wall of sin that separates us from Christ; but the healing and the blessings lie beyond the wall. The path is ours to walk in but Christ cannot walk in it instead of us. The healing is out there for the taking, it is created and it exists, but we need to take possession of it by the power of the Holy Spirit. Sadly, widowhood does not only awaken the spirit in us but also the flesh. The Spirit will speak to our spirit but the devil will point out the needs of the flesh and will groom us into walking by what our eyes see in the material realm, not by the way the Word guides us. Walking by the flesh will keep your wounds open.

The covenantal relationship between a husband and a wife does not originate in human will which by definition (after the sin in Eden) goes against God's will. The covenantal relationship originates in the born-again human will which is in harmony with God's will. A person who has not had a life-changing encounter with Christ cannot behave in a way that is only specific to God exactly in the same way that a born-again Christian cannot live a perpetually sinful life any longer. Reacting to sin by reaching out to the sinner with absolute perfect love is impossible in our own flesh. If it were not impossible, Christ would not have had to die for us because we would have been able to be reconciled to God by ourselves. By choosing to get involved in a relationship with a non-Christian, even though we do not consciously think or say it, what we actually declare is that we are led by our desires, not by Christ – and if we are led by our desires and not by Christ, we are not behaving as a born-again believer and we have not had a real encounter with the Glorious Boaz. When we step into a romantic relationship with another human being, there is a spiritual law that God established – the law of "binding together". There is a serious spiritual dimension to human relationships, because we are not primarily bodies that have a soul attached in a side-pocket but we are spiritual beings primarily, created in a way that enables us to carry out the initial commission God entrusted us with (to steward a material world).

People can educate themselves and they can easily learn to behave in a religious way. A non-Christian can easily adopt Christian behavior if s/he is exposed to the subculture of churches. But Christian culture and social behavior that born-again Christians exhibit are not God's primary focus in someone's life; they are fruit of a fundamental change of self that cannot start by human will, from inside the human heart. It has to be created from nothing, like the creation in Genesis.

I might be scarred and bruised from walking the path of widowhood, but the fruit that came out of those scars is that by the grace and guidance of God I have become aware of the schemes that the devil tried to use to destroy me and I am thrilled to unmask his ways. There might be other ways in which he tries to lure the wounded into alienation from God. So keep your ears open to what the Holy Spirit teaches you – but here is what I have painfully learned about my flesh and the devil's schemes from chasing the Light. No relationship outside Christ will stand. Outside of Him, everything is a mirage that might seem appealing, but in the end it leads to bitter disappointment. There are marriages between two non-Christians or between a Christian and a non-believer that work out – I know many examples – but they still lack the *fullness* of God's blessings and glory. God's love cannot be experienced outside of Him. His care is for His people, just as a parent will look after all the children in the playground – but for his/her own child s/he will look after in a special way. The others might not lack anything, but they will not get to enjoy the abundance and lavish love of the parent. Do not settle for second best by choosing a church attender or a non-believer. The risk is too high, the Bible goes against it and the law of sowing and reaping still applies even during widowhood.

THE LONG TIME CHURCH-ATTENDER

Someone said that attending a church does not make someone a Christian just as living in a garage does not make someone a car. It is a very simple yet effective way of expressing a truth that we sometimes forget.

No one who ends up hurt, abused or divorced believes s/he will end up there. Everyone starts a new relationship with hopes, desires and dreams – and there is nothing wrong in desiring to be happy. God created us for a holy life which originates in Him and leads to happiness.

There is one aspect though that we would be wise to consider: everything has a right timing. Doing the right thing is as important as doing it in the right timing. Truth needs to be spoken in the right way at the right time, when the heart is ready to receive it. A wounded heart needs time to heal. The danger of not allowing the heart to heal before stepping into a new relationship is not obscure, since we all know that healing is a process. Yet we find ourselves sometimes jumping into a new stage which might be good but might not be at the right time.

God is the one who heals and He decides if the right time has come or not. Before entering into a new relationship, the wounded need to re-evaluate their walk with God. They need to rest. They need to catch their breath. They need to learn how to walk with God as a mature Christian in a different stage of life. When I got married I was 21 years old. My walk with God had been great until that age, but as I grew older my personality changed; from a student I turned into a young professional who was married and had responsibilities. By the time my husband died I had to redefine myself as a young adult with a great career ahead, a weird marital status and a relationship with God from which my partner was removed. I did not know what I was like as a young adult woman. I knew what I was like a married young adult and I knew what I was like years before, before I was married - when I was *single*. Now I was *single again* and I didn't know what to do with myself.

The right response when someone is *single again* is not to try to walk away from the singlehood and get into another relationship again, but to learn who they are *now*. The next partner - if there is one - will be chosen by different criteria than the previous one because meanwhile, the chooser has developed. If at 17 the idea of a cool boyfriend is a tattooed rock-star who rides a motorcycle and lives a "happy-go-lucky" penny-less lifestyle, at 45 when a woman is left alone possibly with children and a mortgage, what she needs is a different kind of partner. How will she choose if she does not give herself time to know herself and to know her children's needs? She is no longer choosing only a boyfriend; she is choosing a new parent for her children, a new set of grandparents for her children and a new lifestyle for her entire household.

Especially if in the previous relationship there has been abuse or suffering, a person who rushes into a new relationship is in danger of choosing a partner with a similar psychological profile as the first one. This will only lead to confusion and despair.

Please be kind to yourself and be gentle with your own heart. Please have a fresh encounter with God, learn who He is for the widows and for the orphans and learn how to walk with Him. Being widowed is similar to being shaken for a good few minutes. Nobody should attempt to walk a walking in a straight line in the next second because s/he will be dizzy and will take wrong steps. The worst decisions are taken in the moments of intense pressure. There are some decisions that must be taken urgently, and they should be taken under the Holy Spirit's guidance; but a new life partner is not an emergency even though the proclivity of the heart is to see it as the solution to pain and solitude.

The church is not only made out of born-again Christians because it is not an exclusive clubs for the born again. The Church exists for the benefit of sinners, and sin does not disappear from someone's heart once they walk into a church. A Christian who steps into a broken Christian family needs to be born again and to have a stable walk with God. Unless they are stable and mature in their walk with God, the damage that they will bring in the family is unpredictable. A man who marries a woman who was widowed and takes on the role of protector for her children has to have Jesus' heart towards them because the wounds that they have can sometimes burst out in tears and anger. If the new partner is not mature enough to know his identity in Christ he will become either abusive (trying to control the children in order to prevent them from fighting) or a victim (trying to conform to the description of the previous partner). The sewing together of a broken family needs to be done by God at the right time in the right way, not by a hurt and frustrated widow. Meanwhile, God will prepare a new partner, a right one, if He wants to bring in someone new.

However, the reasons to get married again should never be boredom, sexual frustration, dire financial circumstances, depression or loneliness. The only reason to get married again is the only reason someone gets married in the first place: because God indicates it is the right time - and He points out one specific person.

Choosing a person who attends church does not necessarily make the choice right; a person can go to church in much the same way as they go to a show. The Word of God makes the distinction between a good partner and a bad one by asking us to look at the fruit that that person bears. There are many abusive men who attend church because God is working in them, not because He has finished His work in them. There are many women in church who are rebellious and independently minded in whom God is still working. Just because you find someone in the church parking lot it does not mean they are the right person for a new marriage. It is not like adopting a puppy. The spiritual direction of the entire family will surely be influenced by the person the widowed marries. Do not take this decision lightly, quickly, and soon after the funeral. You are vulnerable and the chances of taking a catastrophically wrong decision are extremely high.

Just because you are widowed does not mean that you cannot *choose* a new partner (if God guides you towards remarriage) and that you have to be satisfied with the "bad apple" that no one wants. There is nothing shameful about being a widow and there is no such unwritten rule among women like "Well, she was married before, she needs to take what life brings now unless she wants to end up raising those children alone!" although sometimes women do act as if this were the case. There is nothing disgraceful in walking humbly with God and seeking an amazing new partner. You do not have to settle for the second best or to lower your standards. No, not "anyone would do". On the contrary, being the new life partner of a wounded person takes a lot of courage and a lot of stability in Christ, and He will only call those women or those men who can stand in their walk with Him as He moves them into a difficult position. It is a challenge to be the mother of children who lost their birth mother. It is a challenge to be the husband of a widow. It was a great challenge for a man to take Ruth as his wife because he also had to deal with Naomi (who now was Mara) and to keep the Jewish tradition of rising up the name of a dead person. The rightful guardian-redeemer of Ruth, the one who took off the sandal, was not good enough; God did not entrust the wounded Moabite to just anyone, He had chosen a man with a good reputation, a great social status and a cheerful heart. He chose the best of the best to look after the humble widow. Likewise, He has chosen His only precious Son for the Church (the Bride). Why would He "bless" you with anything less? God's heart is for you and His blessing will not be followed by any pain –

"The blessing of the Lord brings wealth, without painful toil for it." *(Proverbs 10:22)*

Widowhood does not take away from you the rights of a pure woman because it is not a disgrace or a shameful name, even if you are in a culture in which widows are not protected. God's Word cuts through culture and He is the one who crowns you with purity and grace and wholeness. Do not accept any accusation or condemnation coming from yourself or anyone else. You can rely on God's decrees of protection over you and you can rely on His care for you. You can rely on the justice that He makes for you and if He decides to bless you with a new marriage, make sure you enter into it at the right time, in the right way – and white is still a colour you can opt for your wedding dress because you were not stained by widowhood if you walked in purity with God.

THE NON-BELIEVER

If God guides a Christian to a new marriage, it will necessarily be with another born-again Christian. The Bible makes no exception from this. Christian singles are not allowed to marry outside God's family, and the same rule applies to the widowed. There is no other "rule" than choosing the new partner "in Christ" – in this case, "in Christ" means at the right time, handling it in the right way with the children and stepping into it in a way that is honoring to God and His people; regardless of the looks, the height, the eye colour and the skin shade of the new partner, the marriage *has* to be with another born-again Christian of opposite gender.

The people that the Bible forbids Christians to get married to – and the same rules apply for marriage no.1, 2 or 10 if God takes away 10 previous spouses! – are the non-Christians, however they choose to call themselves (free thinkers, humanists, atheists, etc.). The fact that a non-Christian starts attending church because the person they pursue is a Christian is no guarantee that they will one day be born again. On the contrary, if the only reason they choose Christ is because they *have to*, in order to get a person they desire, chances are that they idolize the partner. The Bible is extremely clear when it says that Christians are not to enter into relationships with non-Christians. The Bible is really clear that we cannot choose to serve both God and the world. The Bible is really clear that idols fall.

The danger when someone is wounded and hurting is for that person to run to whatever option as a partner they find. And the devil knows it, so he plays the best cards he has: a woman who experienced widowhood is in a very vulnerable position and the right moment to make decisions is never under the pressure of pain, despair and emotional wounds. Our minds are connected to our emotions and they have to work together, but until we are healed we cannot rely on our minds to suppress our emotions or to weigh up the options in the decision-making process. (It actually takes a lot of self-control and a very particular type of personality in order to be able to naturally subside emotions to wisdom and take decisions based on wisdom; especially with women, statistics say that under 0.8% of the female population *naturally* choose what they *know* over what they *feel*.)

The danger of choosing a partner who is a non-Christian is that by doing so, we go against the Bible. When we go against the Word of God, we are in rebellion and pride, and God opposes the proud. Instead of choosing the safety of staying under God's Word, we choose the unsafe ground of a relationship that is against God's will. We are not only exchanging God's protection for a safety that comes from a human, but we exchange God's *certain* protection for God's *certain* wrath. Remember, your widowhood is about you and Jesus, not about you and another person. The quality of a new relationship will flow out of the quality of the relationship you have with Jesus.

In God's eyes your widowhood is not an opportunity to sin but to sanctify yourself. You cannot sanctify yourself through disobedience.

No one is saying that there are no well-educated, serious, good men or women who are outside God's family. There are many examples of people who are naturally inclined to raise solid families. A solid family, though, is not the ultimate purpose of a Christian – or, at least, it ought not be. Just because a person is a good person it does not mean that s/he is holy, and what God asks is holiness. God is not satisfied with goodness that comes from the flesh. God wants perfection and He offers it in the blood of His Son. "Good" is not enough for God and it should not be for you either.

At the end of the day, if God chooses that holiness can only be obtained in someone's life if s/he stay unmarried or widowed for the rest of her/his days, then a new marriage is the sacrifice that needs to be placed on the altar. We are called to offer our bodies as living sacrifices to God, not to another human being. Never, never, never trust the goodness of mankind; we are *not* good. We are sinners, born with a sinful nature, without any home. Some sinners choose to do good deeds. And some sinners are saved without deserving the salvation, and they are sanctified without deserving the sanctification. Always, always, always trust the goodness of God – Jeremiah 17:5-9. Always choose the road of holiness, regardless the price. It might seem like a bleak, dark, lonely and depressing path but it is the only way that leads to life. No danger will come near you and nothing will harm you if you choose God's holiness in any season of your life. You are free from any accusation, through the cross. God's call for all of us is always to be and remain holy. And believe it or not, God does not accept any excuses. If you take God's holiness seriously, you will never get bored with it and you will never look for someone to save you from boredom because God's holiness is not a static state of being where everything smells of roses and you sit on a puffy cloud. God's holiness is active and life-giving. It is forceful – but peacefully forceful. If you encounter the living holiness of God, no embrace, no human promise of a lifetime together and no temptation will have any room to hook you because you will be drenched in God's pro-activeness. God is not boring. God is exciting and fresh and abounding in desire to share His life with you. If you are bored in the company of this God to the point where you are tempted to look for company in the wrong place, you should ask yourself whether you really know Him. There is no way you can look into the eyes of the Christ on the Cross and tell Him: "That is cute, that you die for me, but I am looking for something exciting..."

So can you base your future relationship on the sweet nothings, like a naive "possibly - maybe"? No! You are hurt. Maybe more than ever, you need to take God seriously. You cannot allow yourself to be conformed to the pattern of the world because you are not seeking for a worldly solution. You are seeking for a holy God. You cannot reach Him through your own efforts, and striving to re-create around you the same climate your environment had when you were married will not bring you an inch closer to Him. You need to allow Him to bring an end to your married life (emotionally speaking), to bring a closure and to fill you with His power to move on. The last thing you should do is to have someone next to you who drags you in the opposite direction. If you were stable enough to walk towards God alone, you would not strive to justify a relationship with a non-Christian because of the dire circumstances you are in. So merely the fact that you are trying to combine the two lifestyles (your lifestyle which should be holy and the unholy lifestyle of a non-Christian) is proof enough that you are not in the place to take decisions because you do not even know who you are any more. If you knew you were a child of God and you were acting on it, you would not have this issue. If you do have it, there is something wrong in your relationship with God and according to the Bible that needs to be prioritized above anything because that is where your healing will flow from.

"What if s/he were to meet Jesus?" Do not even let that thought come anywhere near your mind. Of course, it is not impossible: God can and does work in spite of our lack of wisdom. But is that something you are willing to risk? What if the person you desire never meets Jesus? What would your life look like? If Christianity were just another religion that has a deity locked in a church, which

you can visit whenever you fancy, of course it is not an issue. You can go to your church and your partner can go to another church; but what do you do when God starts speaking and you cannot box Him in a church any longer and He asks for your loyalty? How do you bring in your contractual marriage (remember, it is a covenant only if it originates in God!) a third party that does not respect the rules imposed by your partner? How can you fulfill God's calling on your life if He asks you to take your family and move to a faraway country as a missionary for decades? Would your non-Christian partner give up security and status and dreams to follow their seemingly mad partner who hears voices from heaven? – The way we see life differs on every single level and goes in the opposite direction to the way the world lives; and if it doesn't, oh dear, there is something wrong! If you think that God will never ask you to do something as extreme as leaving your country and go as a missionary, that might be because you avoid hearing Him and your heart is hardened; He definitely has a plan for your life and a specific call for you. You were created because a plan existed for you – as opposed to you being born and God being taken by surprise and trying to fix a quick calling for this person who He had no idea will appear. And definitely, that call for your life is not for you to build your own little kingdom in union with a non-Christian.

"I will not tell anyone so it will not affect anyone if I get involved in a relationship with a non-Christian." But Jesus knows; and Jesus paid the price for you - and it was a high price. He did not save you and pour His beauty into you so a non-Christian might defile your beauty and the holiness He clothed you with. Nothing in this world is of any great importance compared to your relationship with Christ which is the only thing in your life that truly matters. Money does not bother Christ, but if it becomes your passion, it bothers Him. Christ will be bothered by your potted plant, if that is what comes first in your life instead of Him. If you need to lie about something, that definitely should be quite an accurate red flag for you! (And remember, a lie is not necessarily saying something that is not true; it is also covering the truth or expressing things in such a manner

that they are perceived in a way that is not accurate.) Because we are in a covenantal relationship with Christ, He will constantly pursue you back into His arms, even if that pursuing becomes painful. He will not force you, He will respect your will and your decisions, but He will be chasing you day and night with an irresistible grace. What He did on the Cross for you cannot be undone and the words of obedience and dedication you spoke back in response to the Cross cannot be taken back even by widowhood. Neither funerals nor wrong decisions can break that covenant. Christ will still exercise His right to pursue you even if you use your freedom to run away from Him.

"But there is no one else available other than this non-Christian, I have no other options! I will not allow it to go too far, I just need companion. And even if I fall in love, I will not give in. We are just two friends spending time together." I know all these excuses very well because I have had them whispered in my ears both by the enemy and by well-meaning friends who I dearly love but whom had no idea what they were talking about. Adults do not just spend time together because they enjoy each other's company; they get involved emotionally and they build up hopes in each other. Leaving aside the vulnerability of a newly widowed person, the non-Christian also has emotions and can be hurt. What testimony do we have and how can we look into Christ's eyes knowing that instead leading a non-Christian to Christ we led him/her into emotional deception? If there are no other options but a non-Christian partner, it is because it is not the right time for God to bring another person in the life of the widowed. He will not fail to bring the right person at the right time – and a non-Christian, whether s/he accepts to go to church for you – is *never*, under any circumstances, the right person. The right person will be a mature support and companion in your walk towards Christ; s/he will not become your evangelism project. Christ is wise. He does not call single Christian widows to lead attractive single non-Christians of the opposite gender to Him. You are not called to lead that particular lost soul to the Fountain of Life. Do not let thoughts like *"But s/he is dying without knowing Christ!"*. That might be true,

but it is equally true that we are supposed to guard our hearts! If you truly are concerned about a single non-believer's destiny, who just so happens to be of the opposite gender and attractive, why not get them in touch with a pastor or an elder of the church – someone of the same gender with the non-Christian, who is mature in Christ and sees behind the words? They will surely not be as tempted as you are to be double-hearted and the chances that the Gospel will pierce their hearts are a lot higher than if the Gospel is preached over a candlelit dinner in a romantic atmosphere. Do not think you cannot be rude to someone – if you could actually perceive the great spiritual danger you are in, politeness would be a non-issue, really. Social taboos do not matter when the choice is between life and death. It is not a social image that you are called to defend, but your heart and your life. Whenever the devil tempts you, be it through another human being or your own thoughts, the right response is not a polite excuse, it is not a conversation with the non-Christian about Christian moral values, it is an apparently heartless "NO". It is amazing to me that an increasing number of people have set their faces like flint not to answer the phone in the car while they drive, but when it comes to relationships that will obviously destroy them, they indulge themselves in the sweet company of the enemy. Even if it is not obvious to a non-Christian why a relationship with a Christian is not beneficial to either of them, we trust the Bible and because the Bible says so, we have to have our faces set like flint not to fall into this trap.

Seven or eight months after my husband died, a very popular non-Christian man, who just so happened to be doing well financially and to have a desirable social status and was very stable from a human point of view, started engaging with me in conversations. It was the first one of a series of ungodly men who came across my path and tried to engage with me in more than chit-chat. Non-Christians are not blind. A young woman with no promiscuous past, with good moral values will always be a good catch. A woman who you can trust not to cheat on you is always a good match. Little do non-Christians know that all these qualities they see in our lives are not fruit of a good upbringing but the fruit of the Holy Spirit in us. The corollary of this fruit – which is desirable to any man (Christian or not!) who wants a stable family life – is that we are called to walk in freedom. The Holy Spirit came after Jesus' work of liberation was done on the Cross. And it is for freedom that Christ has set us free. We were not set free so that we would behave as if we were not free! We were set free to use this freedom that we have in Him. The way this "walking in freedom" applied to me when I happened to find myself caught up in an emotional game was that I realized that when I needed to take a decision about getting involved in a relationship or not, the worst possible counselor I can find is the person who is pursuing me or whom I like. I know this now, but I did not know that at the beginning, and I found myself thinking *"Well, this person fancied me for a long while; I need to explain why I cannot get into a relationship with him. He at least deserves an explanation!"* – and I would try to sit down with them, explain the Bible, explain what I believe, try to be open and friendly and positive, maybe even drop in a few lines like *"but you are a great man, I would definitely consider getting into a relationship with you if I weren't a Christian!"* (and sometimes it was true, I would have considered them lest the Bible would have been so particular on this topic!). Bearing this thought in mind, remember where Eve failed: it was not in tasting the fruit, her act of tasting the fruit was just the outcome of her error of engaging in conversation with the devil. That is where her downfall started. So I started being ruthless when it came to my relationship with Christ being altered by people. At the end of the day, Christ himself is jealous for His relationship with me – should I not be jealous for my relationship with Him? I am free not to have to explain to an unbelieving world any of my decisions to enter into a relationship or not. Do not sit down with a non-Christian and try to figure it out together, because s/he has no problem in being in a relationship with a Christian because s/he does not realize what being a Christian means! For them being a Christian does not define someone's life, it is just one component of someone's social life. For us, the power of the Cross is a life-defining, life-changing force that transposes us into an unseen Kingdom. For them, it is a fairytale! Sitting down and trying to explain what you believe is a proof that you do not actually believe it! The things you believe in, practiced for a while, become instincts which you would never even think of explaining. If you believe a particular train takes you to work, you will not sit down with other traveling companions and explain why you are taking that particular train and then ask them how they feel about it. You just get on the train and do what you are supposed to do! Likewise, you are free not to justify your belief but just act upon it. You are under no obligation to explain to a man why you refuse his company – which is why it is so important that you do not flirt with him to begin with when you know for sure that he is not right because he is a non-Christian. If you do flirt with him and give him hope, and then you refuse him, you have a double-minded heart and God hates it. Be straightforward, be pure and be humble. Walk in God's decrees and in His light in all your relationships and He will honor you.

The other very bad counselor you can find when it comes to asking advice about getting into a relationship or not is an over-concerned parent. Over-concerned parents will either try to get you married at any price (regardless with whom) or will try to have you move in with them. People who are emotionally involved in your situation are as subject to taking wrong decisions as you are! The glory of the Bible resides in the fact that it never changes, it is always the same. That is what makes it firm and stable and why God's Word is the only reliable guidance; He is the light and yes, He might use a human being to guide you, but your answers and your eyes are not on people or their concerns for you, but on Him.

I have a trusted friend who is old enough to be my father. Because he is a man and he is married with a woman I dearly love, and he has two adoptive daughters, God used him in my life at a time when I almost crumbled. I was under a lot of pressure generated by a friendship with a non-Christian whom I happened to fancy. It started going in a certain direction. I would keep explaining to him that it is not possible, that we need to consider God (who for him meant nothing) and that I cannot see him again. And then he would call me again and tell me that he would like to know more about what I believe and that he would like just to be my friend, even if nothing ever happens – and so he would get another date with me, and another one, and another one, although he would never call them "*dates*". One of my dearest friends, a Christian cousin over twenty years my senior, tried to open my eyes, but she was gentle and loving, and understanding about my emotions. My conversation with her made me think "Yes, it is not really okay what I am doing... I really should not be doing this..." – and the next day I went out with him again knowing that what I was doing was not *quite* right. My older male friend visited me that afternoon; he looked me in the eyes and said: "*What is wrong with you, are you on heat? However you want to look at what you are doing, it is a sin and you need to stop today.*" – and left. His words pierced my heart and brought conviction and repentance. His words were neither comforting nor polite, nor understanding, nor politically correct. They were sharp and painful – and sadly, true. In the next half hour all contacts I had from that man were deleted, he was blocked on my e-mail and social media accounts and I walked free from the relationship without feeling as if I had to explain him anything at all. My fresh encounter with Christ shaped me back into freedom.

Sometimes we need the Truth to be spoken gently in our lives, but sometimes people focus so much on the gentleness that the truth becomes buried under thick layers of compassion where there should be confrontation. Sin needs to be confronted. You might have a trusted friend who is objective and lucid enough to nudge you back on the trail, but anyone can fail. The only Person who will never fail in guiding you is Christ. You have to work on your relationship with Him as if your life depended on it – because it actually does depend on it. It is for freedom that He set you free.

Now almost seven years after my husband died, I still get phone-calls from well-meaning friends or social contacts who ask me why I have not remarried yet and why is my life *still not sorted out*. I do not linger on such conversations. What is happening between me and Christ in this period of my life is way too precious and important to have the time or the energy required to start explaining or justifying myself. I trust His guidance, I trust His timing, I trust His glory will be revealed in my life whatever the future might hold for me. This place of security, peace and freedom that I am in transcends any human understanding – I really really really should not have this peace and security in my heart, considering the way my life looks like at this point. But the peace that I have is a supernatural gift which I received due to God being faithful to me. If your wounds are fresh and this peace seems impossible for you to obtain, you are right. You are not called to get yourself to that place of peace, you are not called to heal yourself and you are not called to sort out a way of getting a new partner. You are called to follow Him and in following Him with a humble heart, you will receive healing and peace and security. You do not need to justify your walk with him to your peers (– of course, wise council, Church authority and mentoring are a completely different topic, due to us all being under authority). The only thing you need to do is to decide to follow Him regardless of the consequences. His love will never fail you. When you are determined to follow Him, He will bring you to the right place where you can decide to accept the healing over your life, being made whole, and to receive a new life with a new partner or to continue in celibacy. At that point, you will understand that whatever He chooses for you is not only good for you but will bring you happiness and peace and your soul will be satisfied in Him.

CHAPTER IX

JUDGING THE MOURNING

Of all the references in Scripture where God commands about the way His people are to treat those in mourning, I cannot think of a single one that encourages judging the widows. We are not called to judge, and we are not called to share our opinions about situations which we haven't experienced. After my father died, I thought I knew what mourning meant. We also had quite a few funerals in the family after my father's death – in the next year and a half we lost both my mother's parents and soon after that an uncle of mine. Everyone reacted differently and everyone was hurt. Yes, there are clear mistakes that the Bible points out in the process of mourning – like speaking to the dead or idolizing them or creating rituals around their memories – but outside the clear perimeter that the Bible defines as being sinful, which we have gone through in some detail earlier, we have to remember that people are different and react in different ways.

My husband's death was nothing like my father's. It was like the black that I wore after my father's death had a different feel from the black I wore after my husband died. Both were bitter and both were sad; both were heart rending, yet they were different because I was different. A sixteen year old teenager is not mature enough to deal with burying a parent; nor is a twenty-five year old woman mature enough to deal with burying her life-partner. But there is grace in God's presence, and He held my hand both times. His approach with me was different because I was at two very different stages of my life. The words of comfort He had for me when I was sixteen were coming from the same heart as the ones he spoke over me when I was twenty-five, but they had a different shade and a different edge because my pain did not feel the same.

One cannot compare the loss of someone's child with the loss of someone's parent. Burying a child stirs up a particular type of pain; burying a parent is another kind of pain. Burying a partner is a different trial and burying a brother or a sister leaves another type of scar. Just because someone has buried a sister in childhood does not mean that they have the right to judge or condemn a woman who lost her husband while expecting their baby. The relation between the surviving and the dead changes a lot in depth, in intensity and in the experience of loss. We are called to be fruitful, but we are called to bear good fruit, not just any type of fruit. Judgment and seeing ourselves stronger and better than others is, in the final analysis, pride, which does not come from the Holy Spirit. Nothing gives us the right — neither past experiences nor future ones — to use our words to demolish someone. If after going through our share of funerals we cannot find anything uplifting to say to those in mourning, or we cannot teach them what He taught us, it is far better to just keep quiet.

Furthermore, the method God uses in healing one person might be totally different from the method He uses in healing another person. What we need to point the bereaved towards is not a specific method or procedure to follow in order to be healed; we need to point them towards Christ. We have no idea how to heal ourselves — how then could we know how to heal others? If God decides to use us in the process of healing someone else, praise Him! If not, the only thing we can do is to speak the Truth into their lives, help them open their hearts to the Scripture, point towards Jesus. There are certain healing signs that we can recognize in someone's life and we are to look out for those signs, but we cannot, and should not ever force anyone into a healed pattern of behavior.

Soon after my husband died, when everyone eventually started to get on with their lives again, I had a period of time of about three months when I just went to work, came back and locked myself in the house without picking up the phone or answering the mobile or opening the door. I turned off my social media accounts and I just went inside myself and hid there with Christ. There was no second in my life that I was depressed; I was wounded and being an introvert, I reacted like a curled hedgehog. I did not allow anyone in until my wounds stopped bleeding. But I never lost my will to live and the proof that I was on a good way towards healing was that during work I was able to relate to everyone as I had done prior to bereavement. In fact, I started working again two weeks after the funeral and I was as efficient as before. I needed to flood my room and my private life with silence in order to hear God; all my energy in my private time and fellowship with Christ went towards addressing my wonderings, questions and uncertainties with Him. There was a long period of time when I would just shut everything off and sleep, as simple as that; I would just feel that I simply needed to sleep – not sit in bed and cry or stare at the ceiling, but actually sleep - to recover from the trauma, although, in general, I am not the kind of person who is passionate about sleeping.

The same pattern of behavior – complete withdrawal from social life – can be a sign of acute depression from the outside. But if someone is fighting with depression, there are other signs that indicate it. If there are such signs – increased alcohol consumption, developing dependency on substances, inability to think clearly or to carry out minor household tasks, etc., the Spirit of God is still not showing us these issues so we would judge them, but so that we can help them get out of this state of mind.

I cannot even begin to explain how painful it was for me, in my period of recovery, to have one particular person (who, I know, meant well and no doubt wanted to help) calling several times a day and sending e-mails and texts multiple times every day. Introverts do not talk about their feelings but rather sort emotions and thoughts on the inside than exhibiting them and analyzing them out loud. I wished all that nagging had not been there and sometimes the simplest solution is to just ask the widow / widower how s/he can be supported and helped. If someone had asked me what I needed, I would have told them that I needed to sleep and that I would appreciate it if they would stop calling – and I would not have had to unplug all my phones and ban their e-mail address. Sometimes the simplest and most honest way to love someone is to ask what they need. So I encourage you, if someone close to you is going through a painful experience like this (or maybe something similar, like divorce, separation, etc.), just ask what they need. Just doing the shopping for them can help them a lot more than your sermons and just tidying up their house can bring back their will to live. Sometimes pain can be so deep and acute that washing a dish can trigger real hurt and suffering – although it might seem unrelated to someone dying; the two might have washed dishes together and have a great fun while doing it and doing it alone can be more than the surviving partner can bear; we never know. Allow the bereaved to mourn, be Christ's hands and feet in their lives and stand with them in faith for their healing. But do not try to be God or to do His work in their life. You do not know what is best for them and chances are they don't know either, but are trying to find out. Give space and wait with open arms. They might never need you to catch them, but knowing that you are there for them (and not for your "Messiah complex") means more than actually catching them.

Remember, different relationships between the bereaved and the deceased lead to different types of pain, different uncertainties and different questions they might have towards God. Do not try to play God, do not play with the role you have in someone's life and if you cannot help, just refrain yourself from judging. Unless there is sin in their life, you have no Christ-given authority to force on them anything you think they might need. If Christ wants to operate through you, He will speak to you and you will know it for sure. The fruit of your implication in the life of the widowed will be fruit of the Holy Spirit and it will be visible.

The different circumstances of death lead to different reactions. My father died when I was fifteen and what he left behind was not great material riches because he had not had the time to accumulate a lot of wealth – and it was not his purpose to be rich; he wanted God's holiness for him and his family. The few objects that he left behind I cherish and I love because they remind me of him. But they have no intrinsic value; one of them is my music stand that he made for me when I was five and looked like a confused lady-bug trying to learn how to play the violin. I started cello lessons recently, and I still use the same iron stand.

My friend's father's death was nothing like my dad's. Her father left her mother whilst she was pregnant and the first time my friend met her dad was when she was a teenager. He lived a promiscuous life and gambled. But because he had a very lucrative business, my friend had everything she craved – the most fashionable shoes, the latest jeans and all kinds of other designer clothing. She dreaded everything he sent her. When he died, he left behind a substantial amount of money, but that still did not make up for abandoning my friend and letting her face so many unanswered questions. They found him in his apartment weeks after he died, when the smell became unbearable for the neighbors. My friend did not even want to hear about her inheritance, she donated the money right away to charity although she is not wealthy.

Another friend's dad was found dead in his house and they still have not found whether he hanged himself or he was killed.

Although we all went through the loss of our father and we are all Christian women, because it happened in different circumstances and we share the pain of losing our dads, the ways we relate to the events are so different. I love looking at pictures I took with my dad. My first friend does not have any pictures with her dad. The other gets overwhelmed with questions and suspicions when she looks at his pictures. My dad did not leave a great fortune behind; both my friend's fathers left substantial amounts. One of them enjoys leading her father's business; the other one gave away all his money. But the important thing is that we were all able to bring our emotions to a closure and to move on from an excruciatingly painful place. We share in common some questions, but I have questions they do not and they have their set of questions which the other two of us do not. Just as different relationships lead to different reactions in case of loss, so do the circumstances of death. I cannot judge my friend for hating her father's behavior and for not attending his funeral. For her, her father died before she was born and the stuff he sent her was only another reason to feel cheap; she needed him, not the stuff he thought he could buy her love with after abandoning her. If what was in his heart was genuine or not, did not even cross my friend's mind because she was so deeply hurt by his abandonment; everything he did for her meant nothing positive to her. She felt her entire life like a burden to him. Now that he was gone, she finally felt she was no longer a burden to him. My other friend inherited not only her father's business, but his business skills. Being involved in her father's business and taking charge of his affairs brought her closure. She was spoiled by her dad as well, but because he did not abandon her mother, she never felt like a burden to him and her closure did not come by rejecting her inheritance but by taking the same path as her father. Rejecting her inheritance for her would not have meant to finally feel free but to feel guilty for not cherishing her father. We are complex beings and at the end of the day, we have the flesh and the enemy to fight against. We cannot allow ourselves to fight against each other and try to shape each other according to a rule or a pattern we might think God sees for healing. We need a Person, not a recipe for our healing. We need to love and accept each other in Christ because we all, eventually, go through the painful experience of burying someone we love.

We are different and people act differently even in exactly the same circumstances. I am confident that two twin children would relate and react differently to losing a parent because – praise God! – we are not identical. God did not create us to be identical and He does not expect us all to behave in a particular way. He does not want lack of personality; He wants no individualism and no sin – He wants holiness; but anything that is not selfish or sinful is for us to enjoy and to use for our healing.

Be patient with people in mourning. Remember that healing comes in stages, it is a process that starts with a decision, but it is still a matter that takes place over time; after the "sleeping" period I had after my husband died, I felt like traveling around the world. And I did so one year and a half after he died. I visited a number of countries and I was happy to do so alone, but I could not have started with that because I needed to sleep. Someone else might need to travel before taking time to rest or they would feel like moving to another country for two months and travel while resting. There is no recipe. As long as there is no sin, there needs to be respect for the bereaved and there needs to be wisdom in allowing them to have their space. Different degrees of fragility lead to different decisions and different reactions. We do not sin by being fragile, but we might be sinning if we choose to focus on our fragility rather than Jesus and if we choose to live with a victim mentality. Those in mourning need to be helped to keep their compass towards Jesus and walk towards Him. The help that they need is not to leave widowhood behind, but to walk towards the Son of God. The entire effort when someone is drowning is not to be directed towards keeping him above the water but to take him towards the shore. The attention is not on the water but on the shore. Likewise, in motorcycling, the attention of the racer is not on the tarmac that is under his motorcycle every single second, but on the direction he is going towards. By looking anywhere else than the direction he is going towards, there is a high possibility that he will lose control over the motorcycle. In our spiritual walk, our eyes need to be focused on Jesus and we need friends who help us focus on Jesus in dire circumstances. The rest falls in the right place by itself. What the Body of Christ does not need are more know-all brothers and sisters. They are neither helpful nor encouraging and their "wisdom" can prove damaging to those who are hurting. We need to allow ourselves to be transformed by the Holy Spirit and to learn from Christ how to go through suffering and how to help others who are going through suffering.

Christ does not give us the *right* to judge, He does not *call* us to judge. The reason why we are a family is because united, we stand together. It is not that we would become self-righteous with each other. He never asked anyone in the Scripture to sort out someone else. We are called to deal with the issues in our own hearts and to be honest and true with each other. In that honesty and truth we can learn from each other how to become more Christ-like. There is a clear distinction in the Bible about God's heart towards the sinner and towards sin. No one throws out the baby because the diaper is dirty! Widowhood is not contagious; widows do not choose to become widows; widowhood is not an illness. It is a stage of life where much support, offered in the right way that is specific to the widow, is required. The community is there to support widows, to look after them and to rejoice with them in the way God is working in their lives. Yes, there are persons who make an excuse of their unhappiness to sin – be it widowhood, a storm that destroyed their house or a business failure. But God is the one who deals with these issues in their heart. We cannot force anyone – however vulnerable – to choose Christ, but we can speak the truth into life. If we love one another, we will speak the Truth and we will encourage one another in seeking the Truth further.

God's ways are not our ways. We do not know what God is doing in someone else's life. Remember Job's friends – they were well intentioned but they did not say the right words at the right time. They were speaking a general good dictated by recommended wisdom, but the situation Job found himself in was above human knowledge and the solution was hidden from human view. There are secrets that belong to God and unless we desire to do even more damage to someone's life, we need to learn to stand in the council of God before speaking or seemingly to help. If we take on the responsibility to "put back someone on their feet" (I hate this expression, but it is what we all believe deep down, that a widow must be put back on her feet, is not it?), we will surely face sooner rather than later the limits of our humanity when we realize we cannot be God and drag them out of their mourning. If we get someone to start depending on us because we are strong and can carry them for a while, we are subject to falling into a codependent relationship. To this day, I do not know what to tell a widow / widower who is hurting until I ask God the right words to speak into his/her life. The entire concept of bearing good fruit is that we do not create fruit by human wisdom. The right words are formed in us by the Holy Spirit and so the fruit that we bear in our words is good for those who taste them.

We tend to shrink back from words like "prophet" and "prophecies", and considering my family past I understand very well why. Yet the Bible's definition of a prophet is often misunderstood as we associate these words with the idea of someone who foretells the future. In Jeremiah chapter 23, the Bible defines a prophet as someone who stands in the council of the Lord and speaks the right word God has at a particular moment for someone; it does not necessarily need to be about the future. It is a "Rhema word" (a word that is true and actual) in a "kairos moment" (the opportune time). This word is related to God's heart towards someone, a specific word in a specific circumstance. In verse 22 of that chapter we read: "But if they (*the prophets) had stood in my council, they would have proclaimed My words to My people and would have turned them from their evil ways and from their evil deeds." These prophets were speaking about God's love and kindness which is forever true, but they were speaking this truth at a time when that word spoken over a sinful people was only brought forth followed by more rebellion, but I would stress, not condemnation. Actually, the truth that they should have spoken was that God is a jealous God; both God's love and kindness and His jealousy are forever true but what the people of Israel needed to hear was that they remained under God's wrath if they do not stop sinning, not that they are loved. His love was manifested towards them by urging them back from under His wrath: God never ceased to love them, but His love needed to be spoken in a way that would have pierced their hearts not in a way that would have comforted them in their sin.

It is extremely important when we speak to a widow(er) that first we stand in the presence of the Lord. It does not have to be a week of fasting and praying, it is enough to ask the Lord on the spot: "Lord, what do you want me to say NOW?" and to open our mouths trusting that He will fill it with His words.

The Scripture which encapsulates the essence of my experience with God as a widow is James chapter 1, verses 12-19:

"Blessed is the one who perseveres under trial because, having stood the test, that person will receive the crown of life that the Lord has promised to those who love him. When tempted, no one should say, "God is tempting me." For God cannot be tempted by evil, nor does he tempt anyone; but each person is tempted when they are dragged away by their own evil desire and enticed. Then, after desire has conceived, it gives birth to sin; and sin, when it is full-grown, gives birth to death. Don't be deceived, my dear brothers and sisters. Every good and perfect gift is from above, coming down from the Father of the heavenly lights, who does not change like shifting shadows. He chose to give us birth through the word of truth that we might be a kind of first fruits of all he created."

Our desire to know what God was keeping away from us has conceived and gave birth to sin. Since then we have been rolling down on a spiral of confusion and death. In spite our rebellion, God gives us perfect gifts – among which, families. Yet, our treasured partners or children or parents are not safe from the condition of humanity as we know it today. The only way to break out of this chain of events repeating in each generation is not by trying harder to change the consequence of sin, but to go back to the root and change the cause of it: our hearts.

The greatest blessing we have available is the Holy Spirit who can live in us: He can teach us how to leave the old self behind and once with it, pain, death and anger will be forgotten. However, the old self has to experience death and it can either experience it alone, or with Christ through His cross.

My hope is that we stop fighting our emotions or our circumstances and go to the cross with the mess we created. There, we can forget all the past, all the pain, the illness and death, and step into a different kind of life: one full of light and perfect gifts. He does not, will not change: He is lovingly waiting for us to turn to Him.

FINAL WORD

One of my friends has recently asked me if writing a book like this has been in any way emotionally taxing. I never asked myself this question, but as I was thinking what to answer I realized that more than it was emotionally taxing to write it, it was to read it when it got in its final form.

It's emotionally taxing to think about all the places I have been with the Lord – all the valleys, all the shadows, all the dangers. It is taxing to follow Him. It is taxing to push our beings beyond our limits. Just because Christ has broken through the canopy of sin, it doesn't mean that we're not fighting against principalities. We are victorious in Him, and we know that. But even victors get hurt and wounded. There's no such thing as a cheap victory.

The church needs more conviction. The church needs repentance. The church needs to turn away from tradition. The church needs to learn to let the dead bury the dead. We are the light of the world and we are the salt of the world. If we lose our capacity to shine and our capacity to give taste to this world, what hope is there left? We underestimate how vital we are to the world. We are not the salvation, but we know the way to salvation.

Pain can turn into slavery. We need to undress, church. We need to go back in the presence of God, brokenhearted and beaten and bruised and to face our God. Just because we are in a time of relative economic stability, He has not changed and neither should our awareness of our need of Him. His arms are always open, always ready to heal, and always ready to send us out in ministries. The point of it all is to show the world a life worth living. Other than Christ, there is no point to live and no hope in death.

Why am I writing this as a final word in a book written for widows? I am writing this to widows and widowers because the point of receiving healing from our Father is not the healing in itself, but the advancement of the Kingdom. Widowhood, pain, happiness, joy – nothing changes the great commission.

Some of our wounds are present in our lives because we made bad choices. Other wounds are in our lives because we have been sinned against or we have sinned against others. Regardless, Christ can and will use them, should we choose to allow Him to. It will be emotionally taxing, of course. But there is no way of giving ourselves to Him other than actually giving ourselves to Him, regardless the cost; when we give ourselves to Him, He will use us. Our Father's house does not have hangers.

Be blessed.